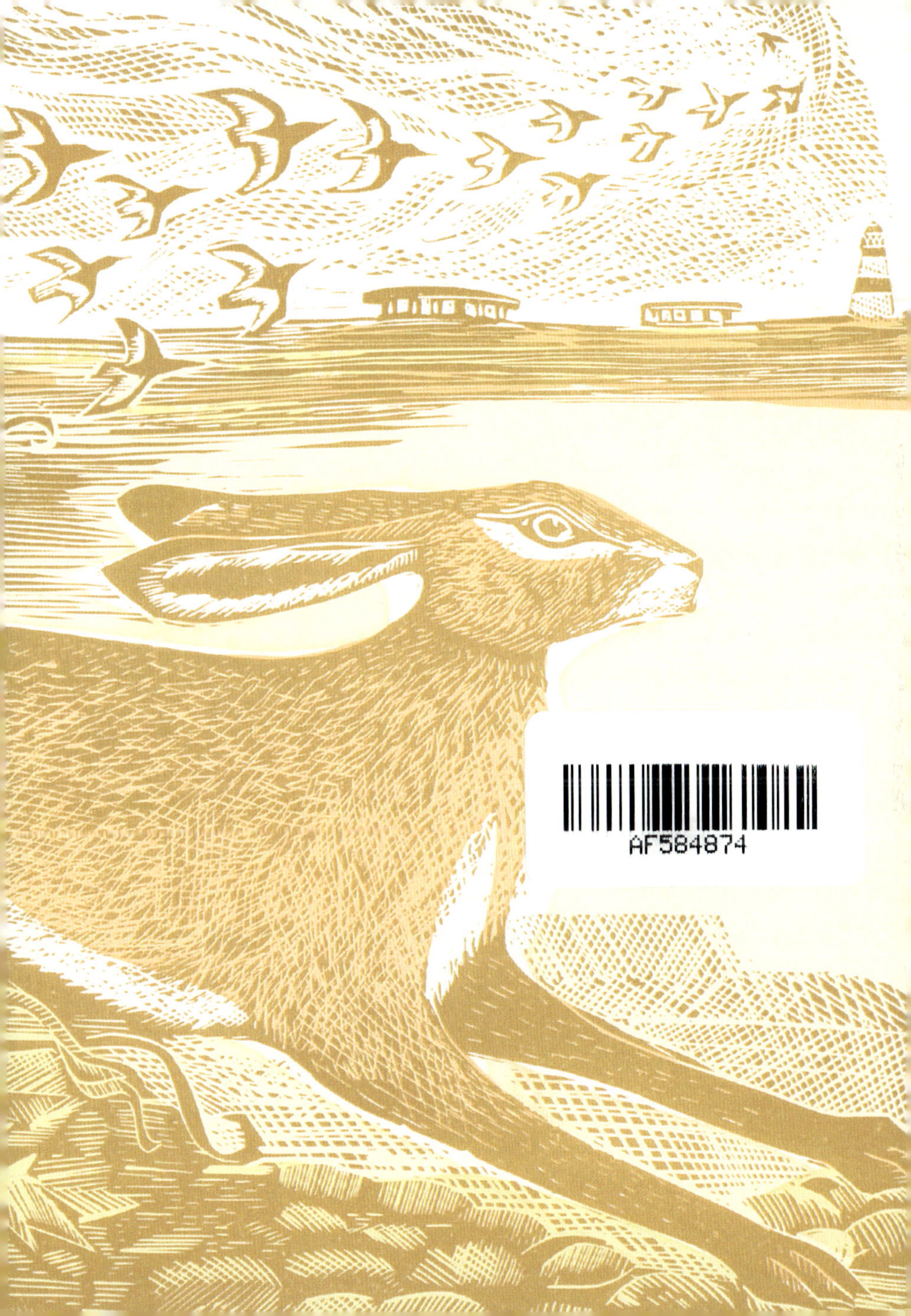

SPRING UNFURLED

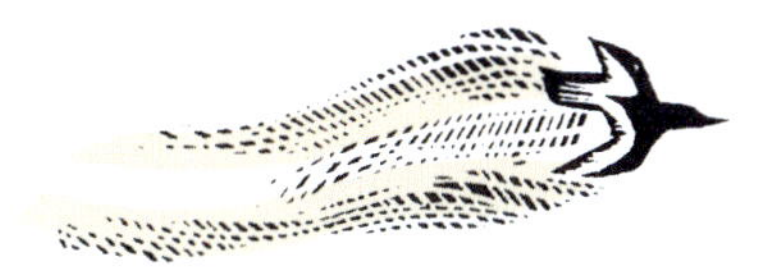

SPRING UNFURLED

ANGELA HARDING

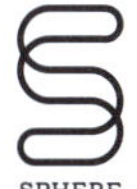

SPHERE

SPHERE

First published in Great Britain in 2025 by Sphere
3 5 7 9 10 8 6 4

A CIP catalogue for this book is available from the British Library.

ISBN 9781408721919

Project Editor: Helen Brocklehurst
Production Manager: Abby Marshall
Cover and interior design: Ben Prior
Typeset in Spectral Light
Printed in Italy by Printer Trento Srl
Papers used by Sphere are from well-managed forests
and other responsible sources.

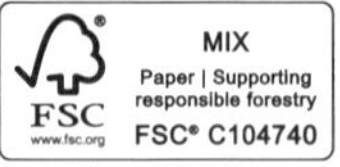

Sphere
An imprint of
Little, Brown Book Group
Carmelite House
50 Victoria Embankment
London EC4Y 0DZ

The authorised representative
in the EEA is
Hachette Ireland
8 Castlecourt Centre
Dublin 15, D15 XTP3, Ireland
(email: info@hbgi.ie)

An Hachette UK Company
www.hachette.co.uk
www.littlebrown.co.uk

For my Father

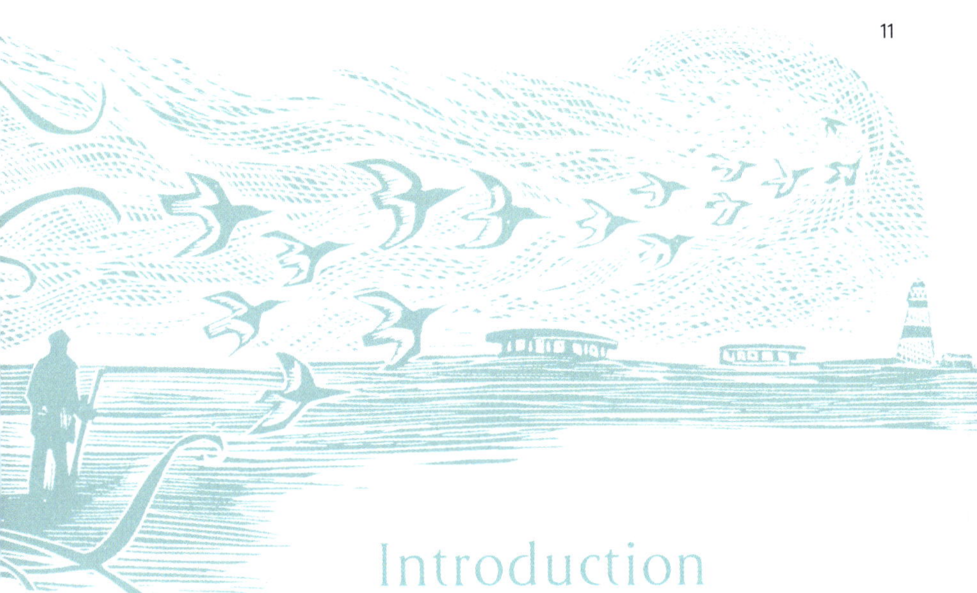

Introduction

Seasonal change has always been a great inspiration for my artwork. I love the changing light that brings new colours and smells. The seasons are nature's clock, bringing birds from distant shores to nest and breed in our gardens. Then, when the days shorten and evening air is chilly, they know it's time to leave. Over my lifetime there has undoubtedly been a change in the timings of when these migrants appear and disappear and we are all aware of climate change and the effects on nature. This changing world reflects in our wildlife, the countryside and with the seasons. It is the seasons that mark time and the passing years; we remember the winters with snow and the summers that let us dine outside and the late spring frosts that wipe out seedlings. Each season has its own unique aspect: winter's watery light, autumn winds and colours, the joy of long summer days and spring's full force of green growth bringing regeneration.

So it is hard to say exactly when one season stops and the other begins; the changes are not necessarily gradual but come in fits and starts. Seasons have no regard for the official times written down in a calendar. Spring, more than any other of the seasons, is like this. Perhaps this is because in the darkness of the winter months, we long for it to begin before nature is really ready. It cannot be called spring when the rooks start to gather sticks for their high tree-top nests, or the first glimmers of aconite and crocus leaves push through the frozen ground, but it feels like a little bit of spring is starting. Early spring is very different to the full-force frothy green of spring proper; it is understated, it is bare branches, it is the blue-green leaves of white glowing snowdrops and hellebores, but spring at all is stages has an energy that engages us with the outside world.

Opposite:
Orford Hares
(Linocut and silkscreen)

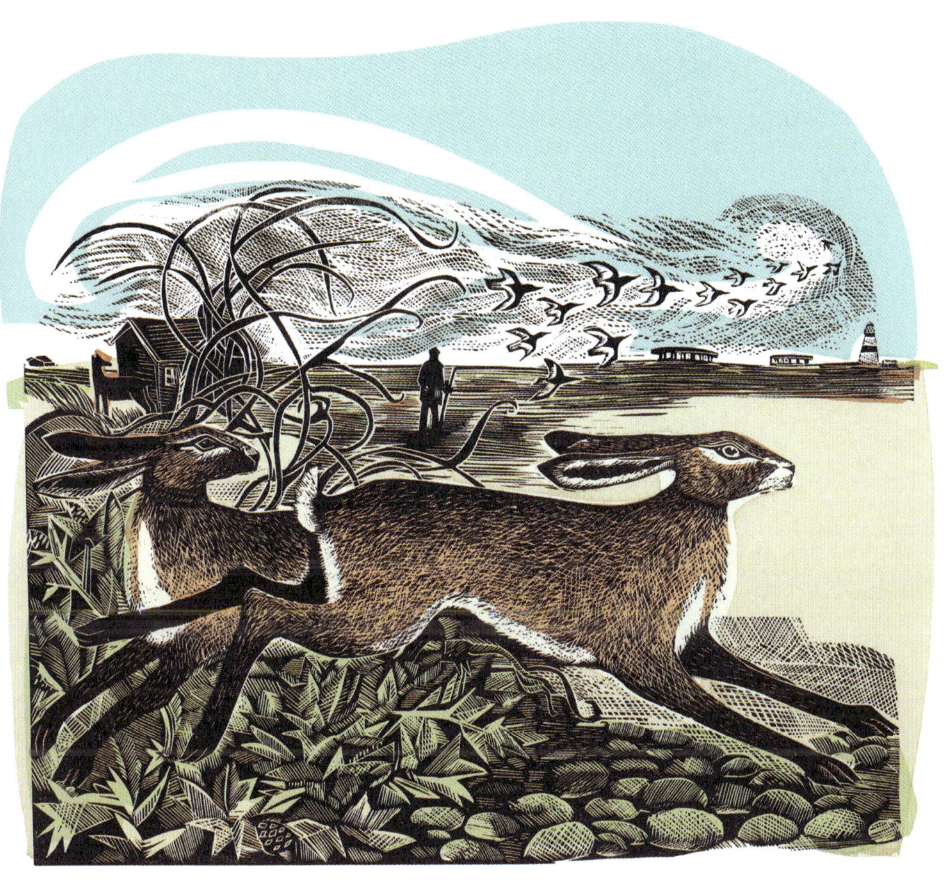

Spring Unfurled is the first in a series of four books that reflect on the seasons. This quartet has its origin in my first book, *A Year Unfolding*, which is a printmaker's view of the changing seasons, though I have added some new images and text to my original thoughts about this season. And this new small, collectable format works so well with my artwork. It is a small book that you can put in your pocket to muse on travels and times alone, or a gift book to share with others who also love nature.

The other books in this series are *Summer's Hum*, *Falling into Autumn* and *Winter's Song*. I hope you enjoy them.

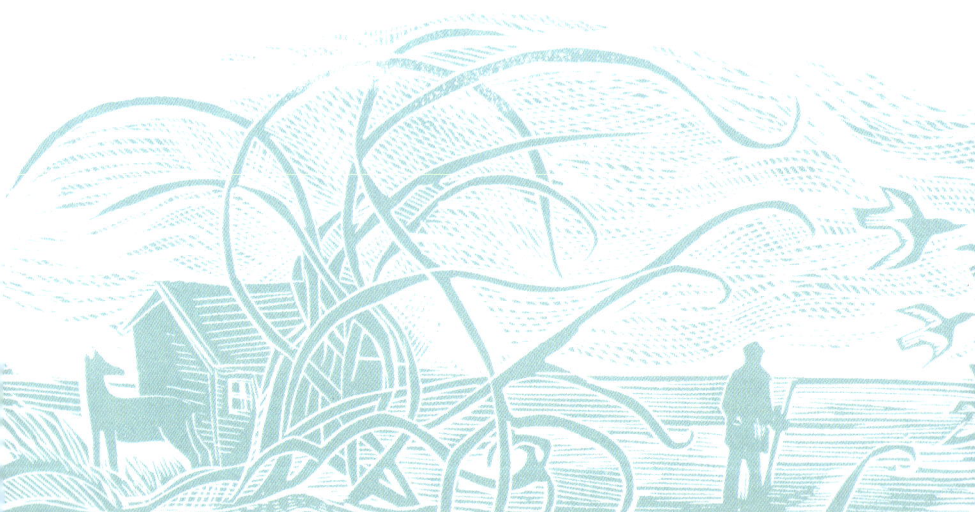

I can't remember where I heard it, but I was once told that Valentine's Day – 14 February – is the official day for birds getting together. So, I think Valentine's Day should be called Nesting Day. I am not sure this is true, but it is certainly very noticeable that blackbirds start to pair up around this time. The males start to defend their territory, their beaks seem to become a brighter orange and there is generally a lot of showing off.

Opposite:
Early Nesters
(Lithograph)

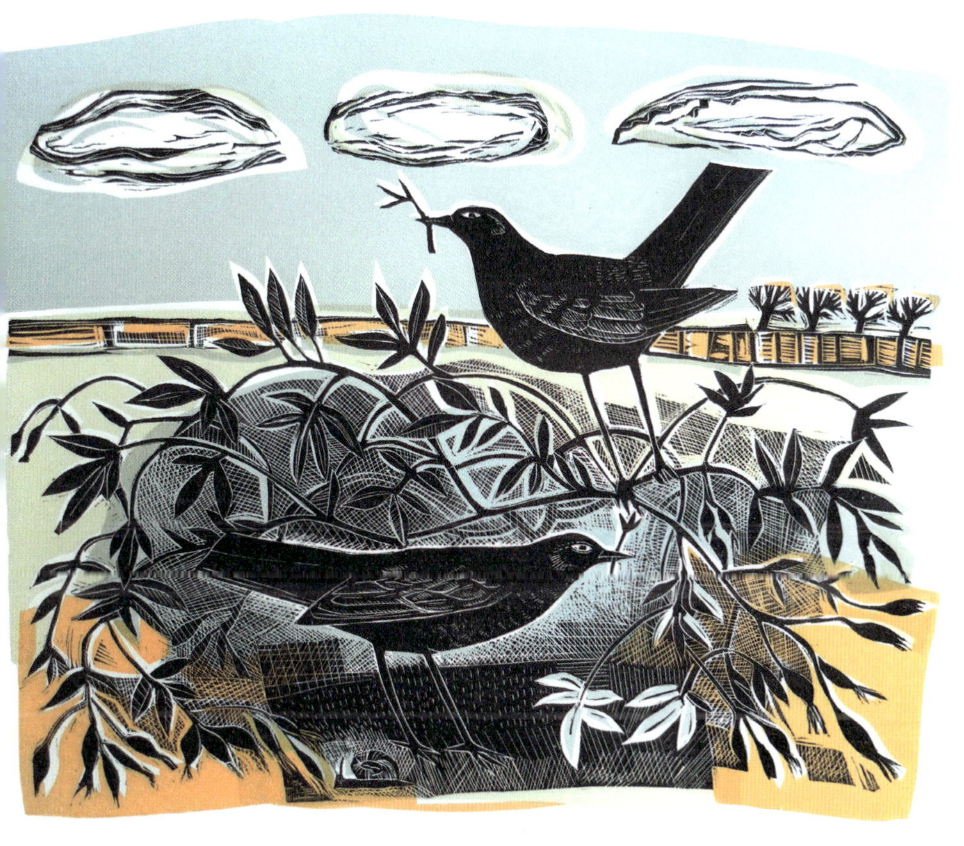

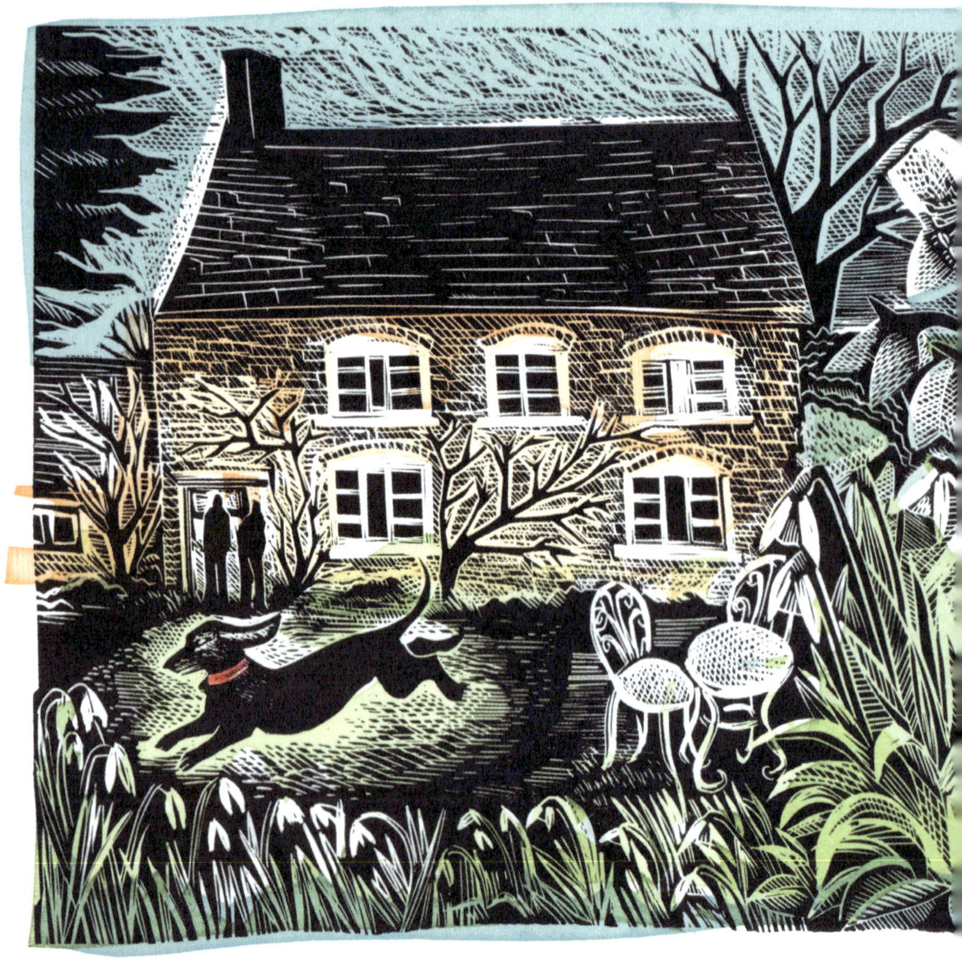

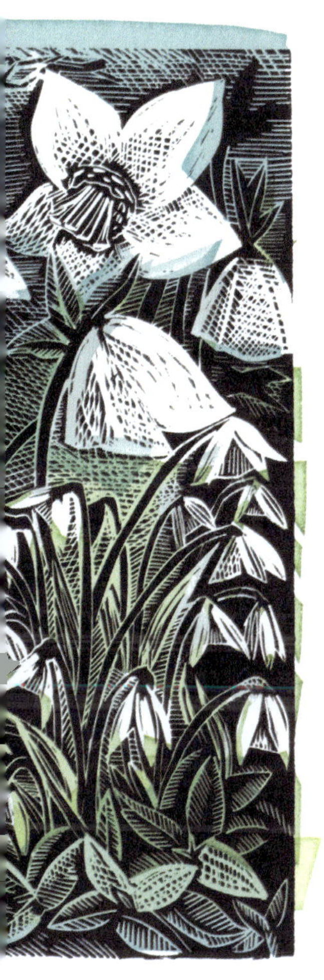

This print was commissioned by Andrew Jones, who is Head Gardener at Deene Park in Northamptonshire and lives in this beautiful cottage. I have tried to capture that feeling of early spring, of the joy of the first flowers appearing in the garden. Along with the crowd of snowdrops, the tall, larger white flowers are my interpretation of hellebores – also known as the Christmas rose. It is one of my all-time garden favourites and I have a large patch of them in my own garden. They are not only white but soft pinks with spotted centres, lilacs, and some wine-dark purple ones with yellow centres. Their nodding heads shimmer in the cold winds of this season and their leathery, glossy green leaves can withstand the winter frosts, giving the garden colour when it is most needed.

Opposite:
Gardener's Cottage
(Linocut and silkscreen)

Waking to see the first light of a spring morning is, for me, the best way to start a day. Our bedroom has a beautiful view of rolling hills, sheep fields and gardens. Through the window you can also just about see the top of my studio roof. Behind the studio, the fields slope down to a valley that has a small stream which snakes through the valley bottom. On cool spring mornings, the drama of a 5 a.m. start is aided by the valley mist thrown up by the stream. The bands of thin cloud turn the trees into just visible fingers that poke through a curtain of fog. On these mornings, the colours are so beautiful: rose pinks slanting into slate grey and soft blues, a watery palette of softness that means it is going to be a beautiful day.

Opposite:
Spring Tulips and Lambs
(Linocut and silkscreen)

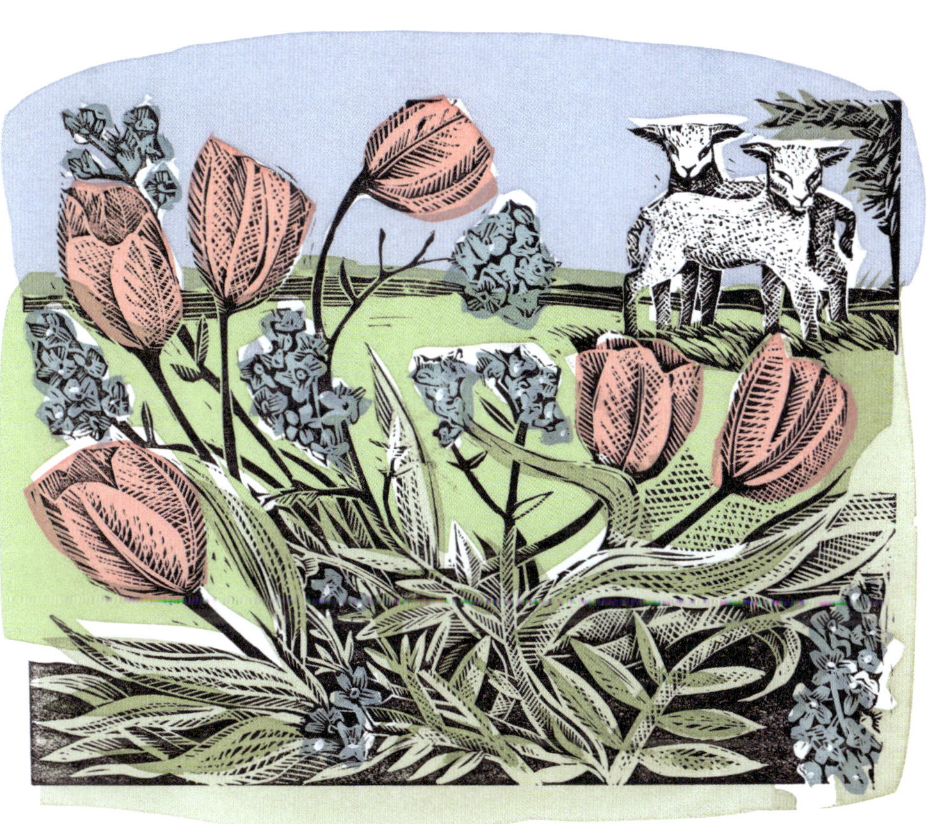

My studio is at the bottom of my garden. It looks out into sheep fields and farmland; it is where I watch birds. The birds I see are the now numerous red kites that glide past my window on the lookout for carrion, acrobatic swallows and the bobbing dance of pied and yellow wagtails.

Opposite:
Wagtails and Daisy Fields
(Linocut and silkscreen)

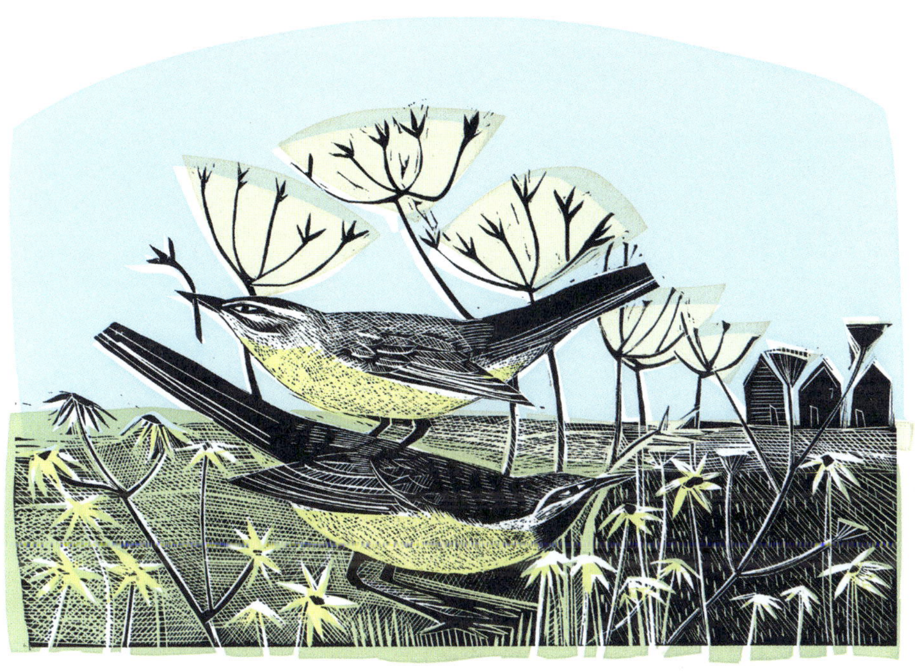

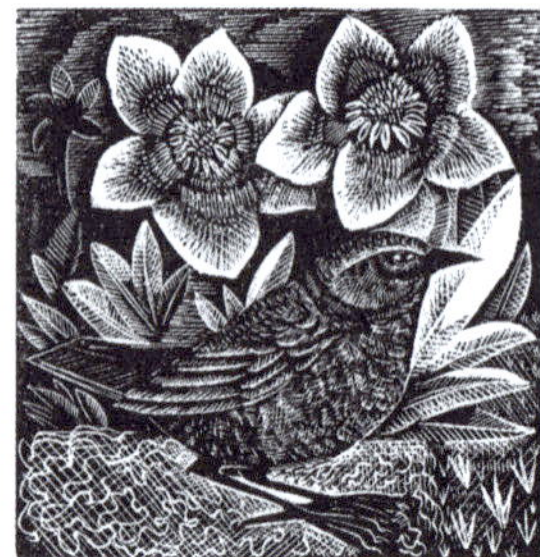
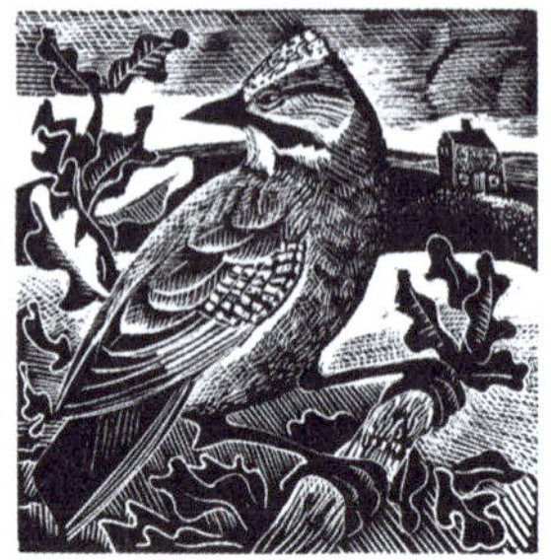
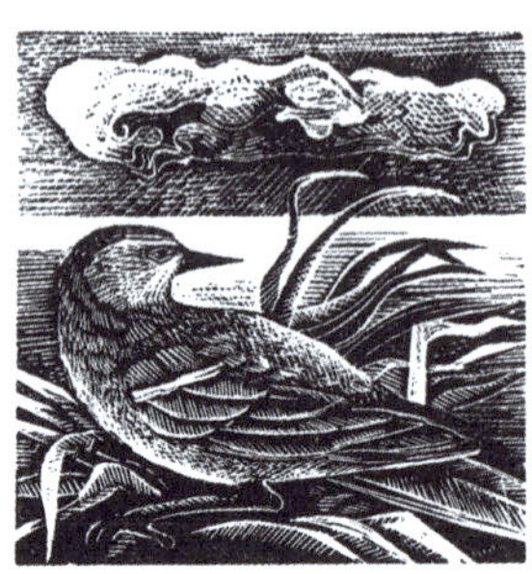

There is nothing that announces spring more strongly than the dawn chorus. By the time of the official spring equinox, the volume of bird song is loud enough to wake you up – you know that spring has arrived. The dawn chorus is multi-layered: an undercurrent of the dull, soothing rhythm of wood pigeons; layer two is the sharp, shrill, unbelievably loud wrens, with dunnocks, chaffinchs, great tits and blue tits adding their song on top; and finally the best layer of all, just below our bedroom window – the clatter chatter of the house sparrows.

Above:
Dunnock, Jay, Warbler
(Wood engravings)

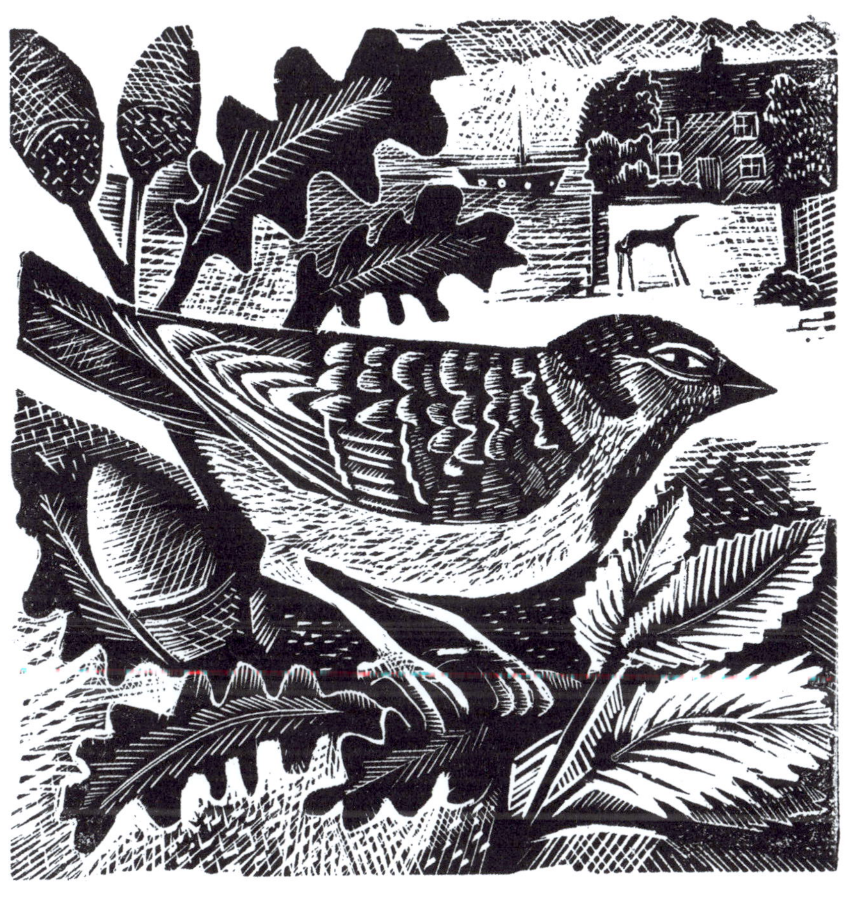

Above:
House Sparrow
(Wood engravings)

In our garden we have a very tame male blackbird, named Bert. He is my gardening companion and comes closer to me than any of the robins. When I am digging he will come so close you could almost touch him – he cocks his head to one side then, quick as a flash, darts in at my feet to collect worms and any other tasty thing he has spied in the soil. Bert has the remarkable ability to sing while still having a mouth full of food for his young. Male blackbirds look after their young for longer than the females. Bert is a great single dad.

Opposite:
Spring Blackbird
(Linocut and silkscreen)

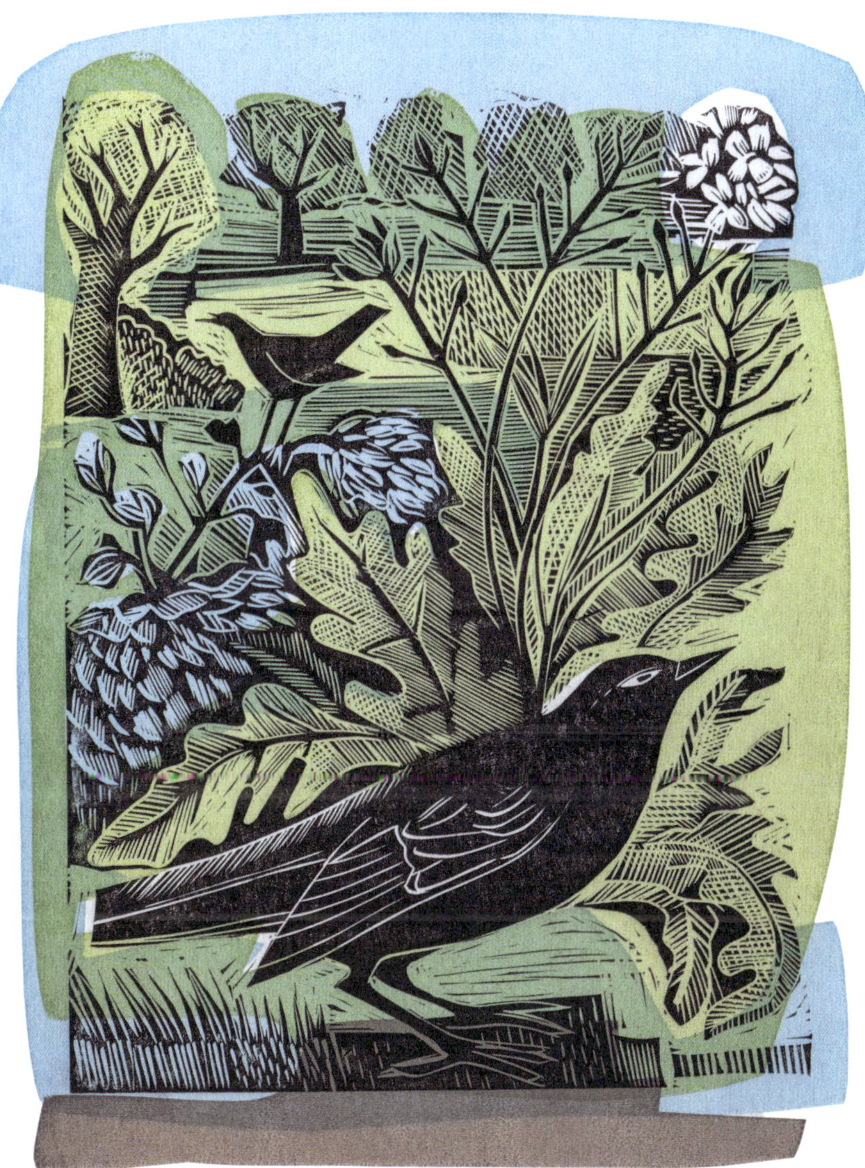

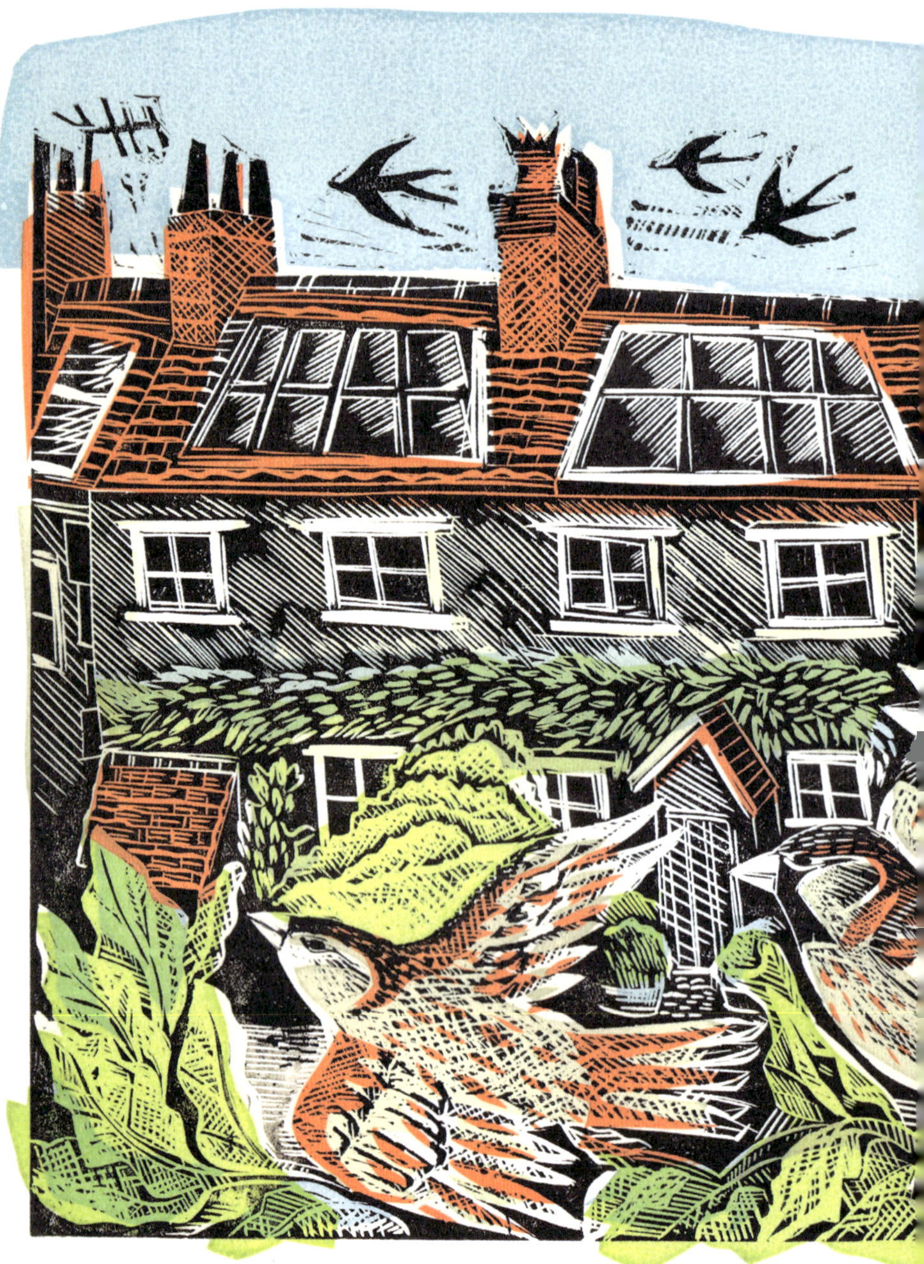

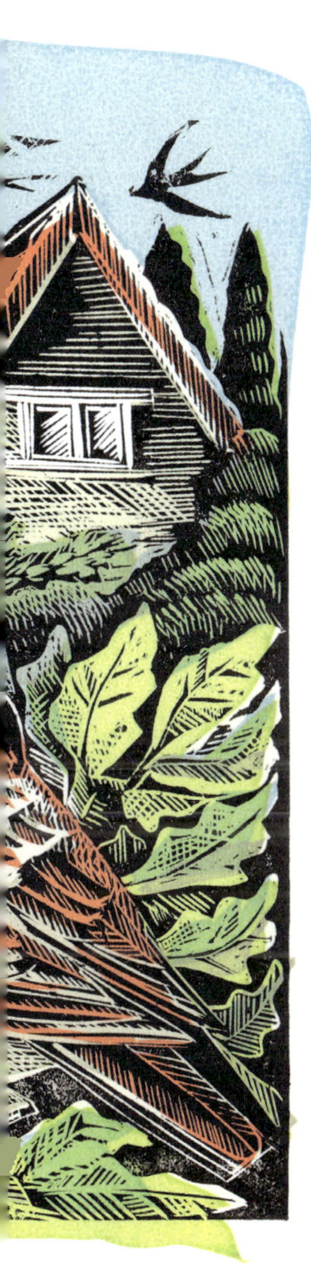

The house sparrows live in the thick ivy that climbs up the front of the house and keep us entertained throughout the year with the lively discussions they hold amongst themselves, of the pecking order in their group and their great love of dust baths. I love them dearly and they are very much part of our home.

Opposite:
House Sparrows
(Linocut and silkscreen)

At the front of our house there is no porch. The front door opens straight into the sitting room and there is always someone coming or going so the door is constantly banging shut. It was therefore very surprising when one of our resident blackbirds decided to nest in the climbing rose which trails over the front door. She seemed very happy and not disturbed by the banging of the door or the fact that our faces were often peering through the branches to see how she was doing. I am pleased to say she raised her brood successfully and has returned a number of times.

Opposite:
Blackbird and Rose Nest
(Linocut and silkscreen)

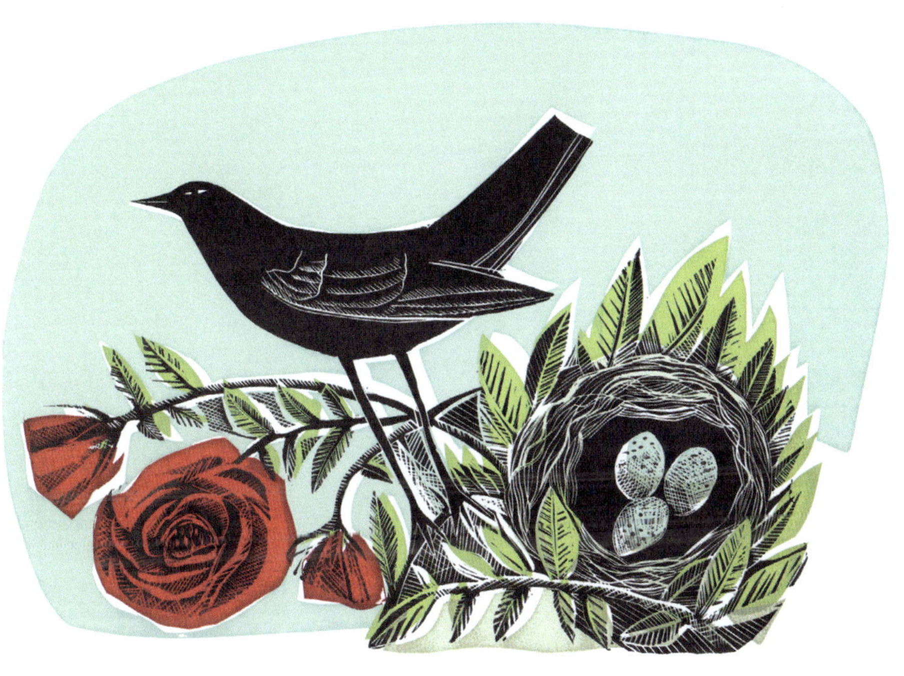

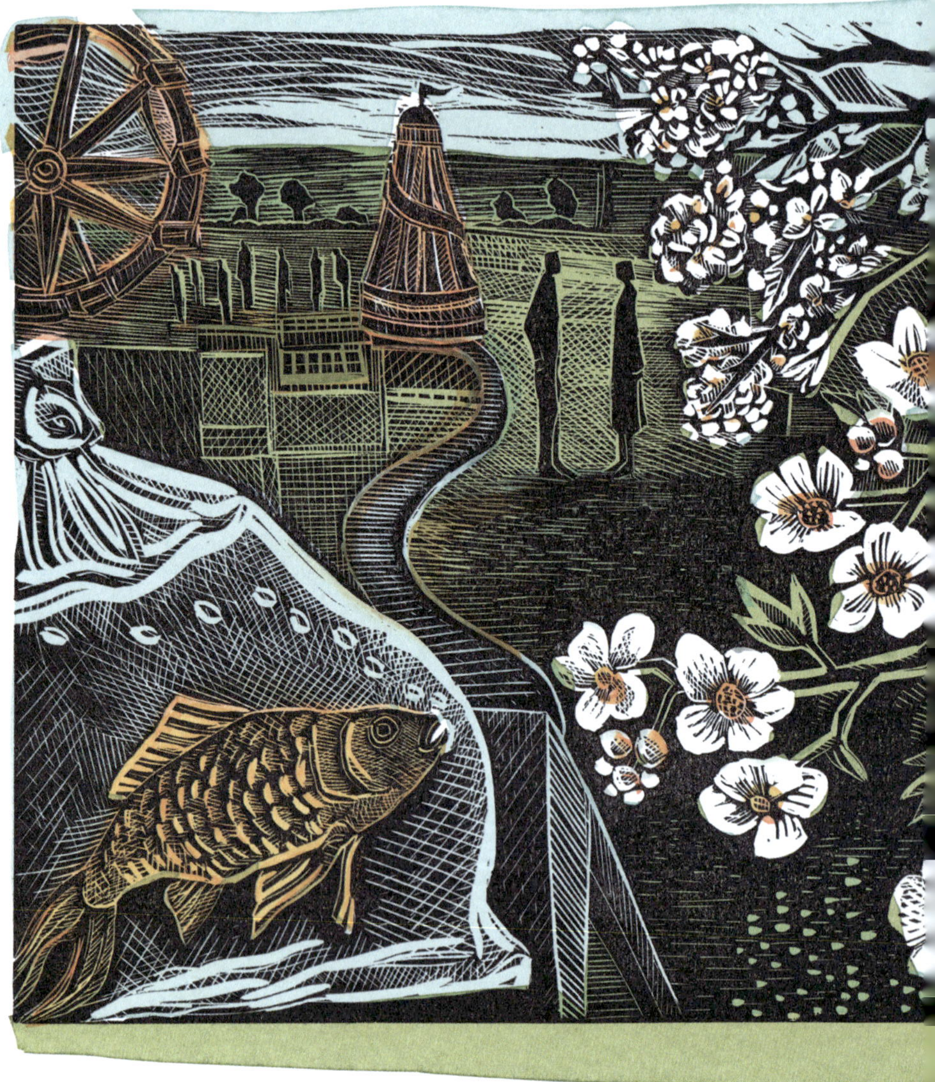

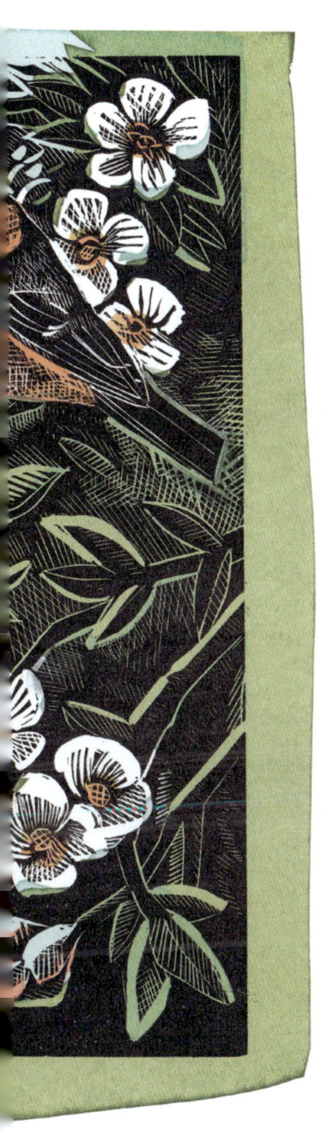

In March every year my children used to insist on going to Uppingham fair. It always seemed to rain on the evening we went to the fair, it was always cold, and we always came back with a goldfish – which inevitably I ended up having to look after. But then Frank, a fellow village resident, would come to the rescue. Frank has the most beautiful garden pond and can make goldfish thrive. I don't know how many goldfish he kindly accommodated, but after the traditional trip to the fair came the Born Free moment. The children would take the hard-won fish round to Frank's garden, where it would undoubtedly have a better life and a much better chance of survival.

Opposite:
The Goldfish Pond
(Linocut and silkscreen)

This illustration represents the start of my gardening year. I always start the year with the thought that this is the year I will have a weed-free garden! But of course, it never happens – I have too many artwork deadlines and trips away to ever have the garden looking as I would truly like. I expect all gardeners feel the same. However, the untidiness of my garden does bring the benefit of hiding places for hedgehogs. I have included two yellowhammers in this image. We are very lucky that they still tumble down the local lane in a bright flash of yellow, as while they were once very common in the UK, they are sadly no longer as prevalent.

Opposite:
Wonders of Weeding
(Linocut and silkscreen)

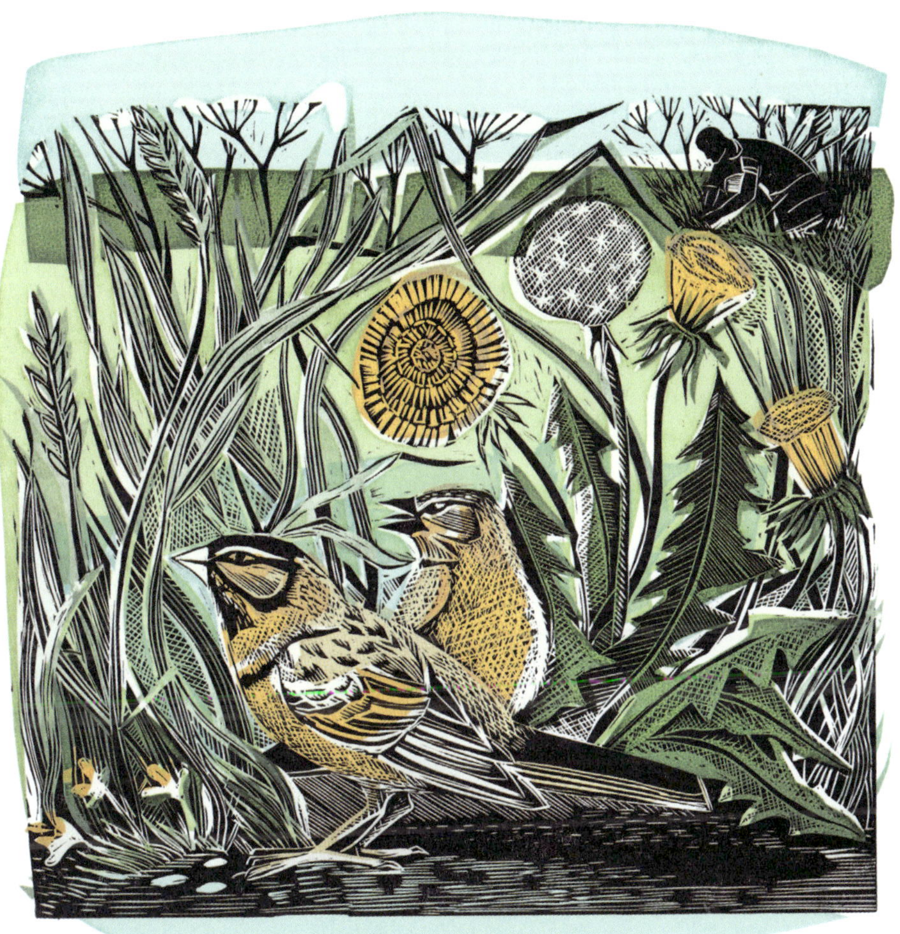

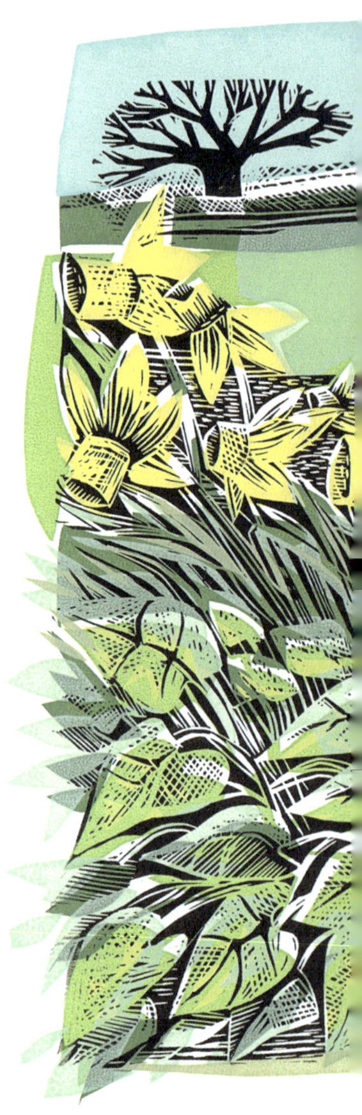

Over the years we have owned a number of sighthounds – part of our daily routine is walking the dogs. As our whippets are getting older, walks are not as long as they used to be, generally around the village or down muddy lanes and across the fields to home. I make sure to keep them on the lead in springtime. Many birds nest on the ground and so are particularly vulnerable to disturbance from walkers, cyclists and dogs. Keeping to paths and having dogs on leads in nesting areas can make a big difference to the success of a breeding season.

Opposite:
Look Out
(Linocut and silkscreen)

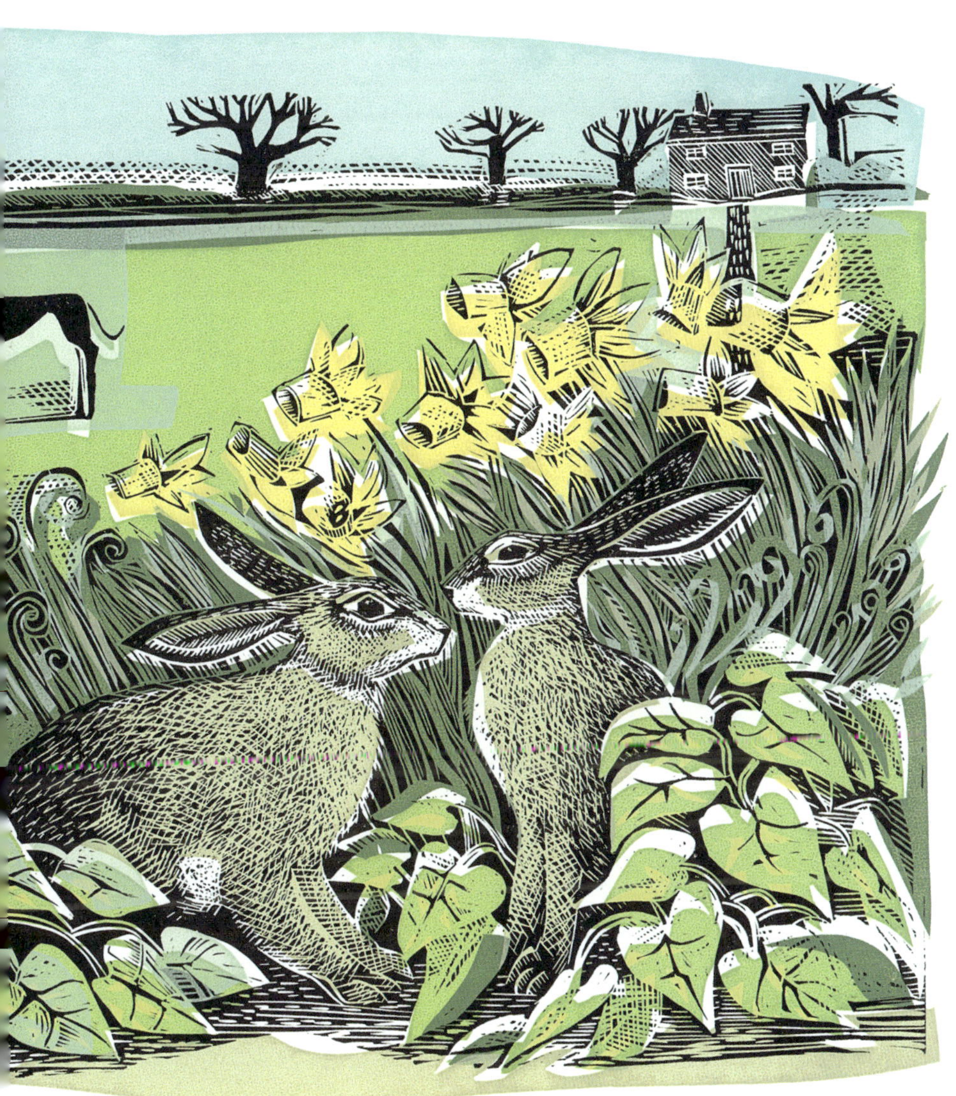

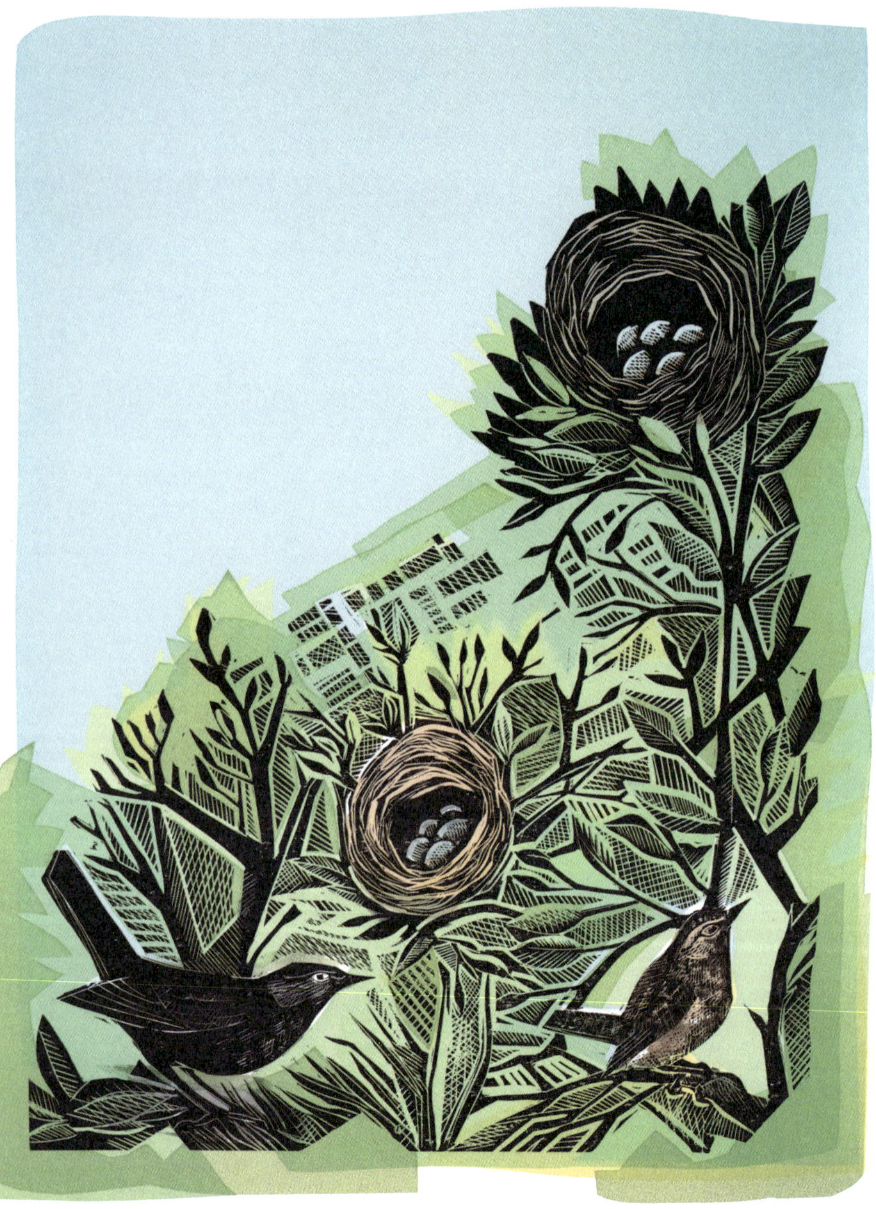

Opposite:
Spring Nesting
(Linocut and silkscreen)

Birds inspire many of my images in spring with their beautiful songs and dashing flight to mate and build their nests.

At one time, it was thought by the residents of the village of Marsden in Yorkshire that they could stop the return of winter by capturing a cuckoo. It is a strange coincidence because my home village of Wing has the same myth. Because of this, the villagers of the past were known as 'Wing Fools'. Perhaps this same story is being told in villages all around the UK.

Opposite:
Cuckoo
(Linocut and silkscreen)

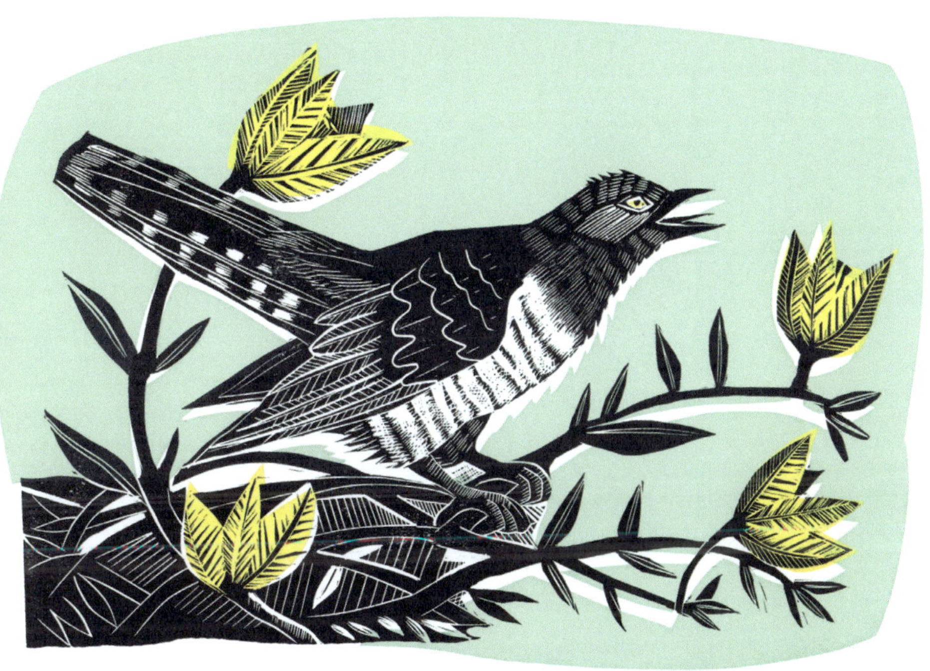

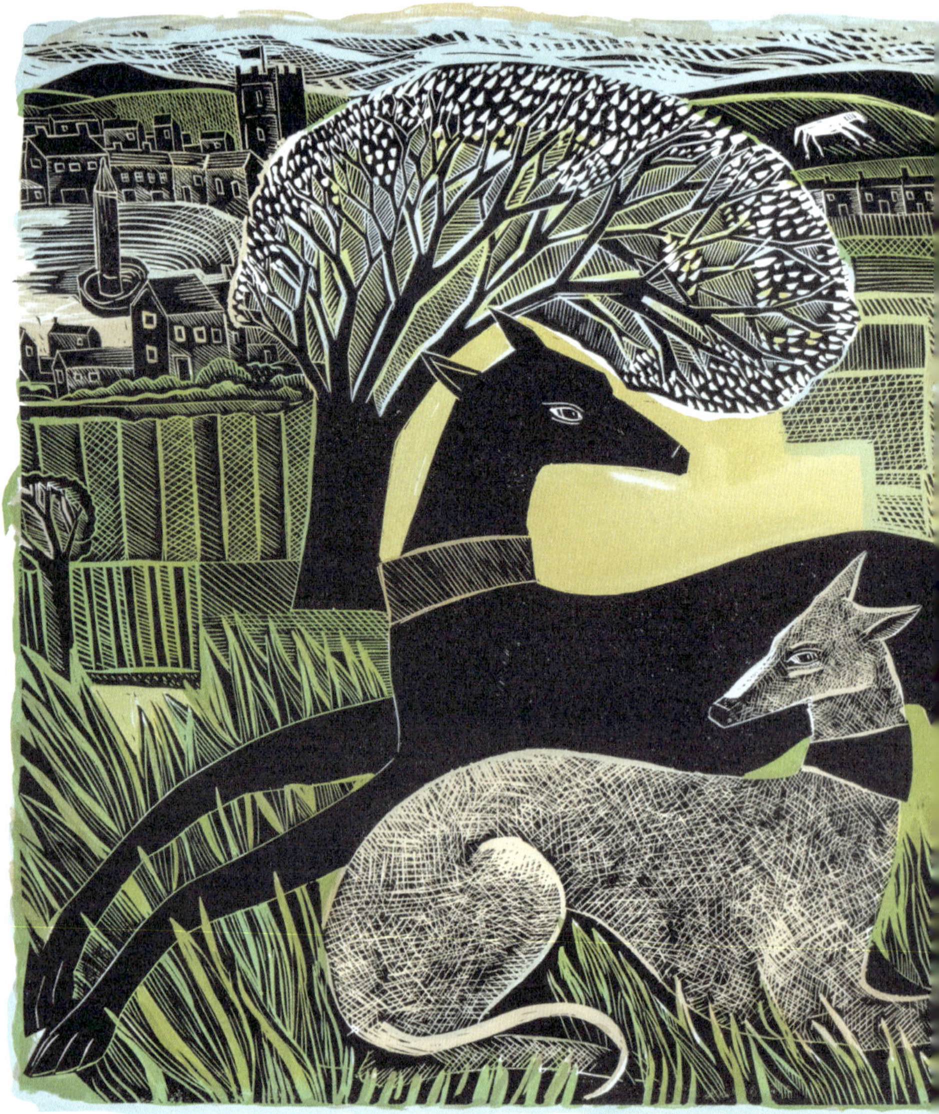

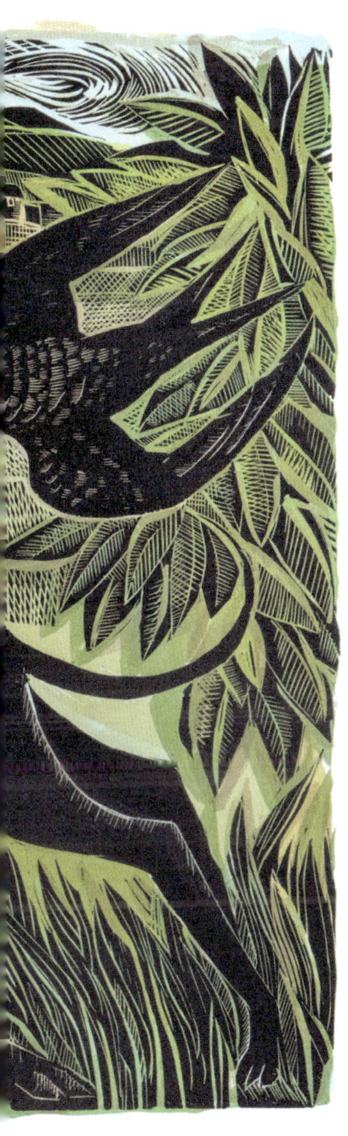

When I was a very young child my family lived in Richmond, North Yorkshire. This print is a memory of that time and the home we had there. The background landmarks in the print of the White Horse and marketplace still echo with the sound of screeching swifts. But it is the garden that I remember best - particularly the cherry tree. In springtime, its branches would bow down heavy with blossom.

Opposite:
Two Yorkshire Whippets
(Linocut and silkscreen)

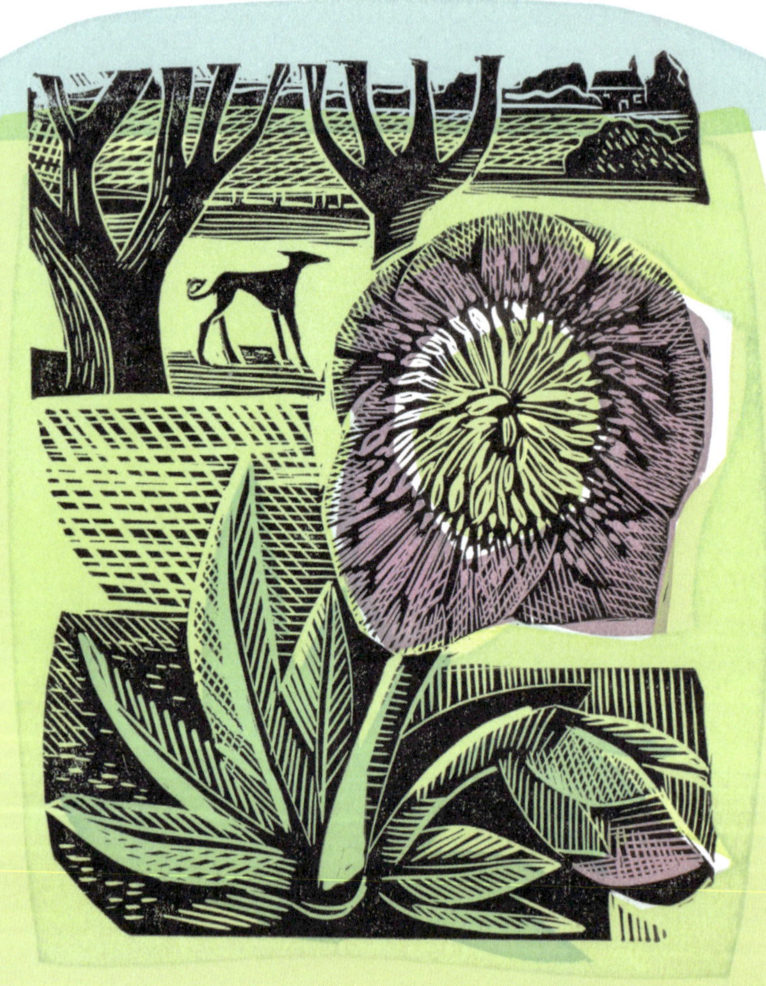

For many years I produced a monthly editorial illustration for Gardens Illustrated magazine. In this one, I used purple spotted hellebores from my own garden in the foreground and incorporated Amy, our little black whippet, in the background. These flowers do not usually tip their heads to the sky, so I have used a bit of artistic licence to highlight their speckled pattern that I love so much. They are a promiscuous flower, so when the seedlings mature they will often have cross-bred, mixing the whites, pinks, purples and spots of their parent plants. You never know what you might get!

Opposite:
Hellebores and Hound
(Linocut and silkscreen)

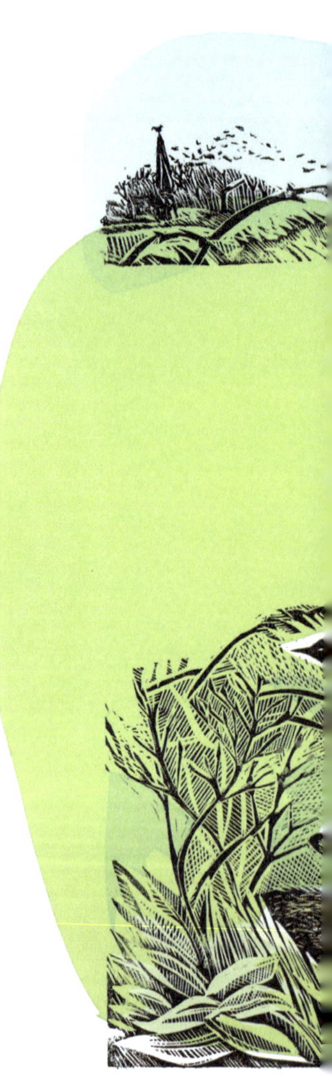

April brings in blackcaps and the chiffchaffs return; this is another sign of spring. High in the branches the chiffchaff is chirping out its name in a short, staccato rhythm. Its song is rather flat and dull when compared to the tumbling melody of the blackcaps. The blackcap's song is so beautiful it is worth just stopping and listening to; it has been compared to the sound of tumbling water.

Opposite:
Spring Hedgerow
(Linocut and silkscreen)

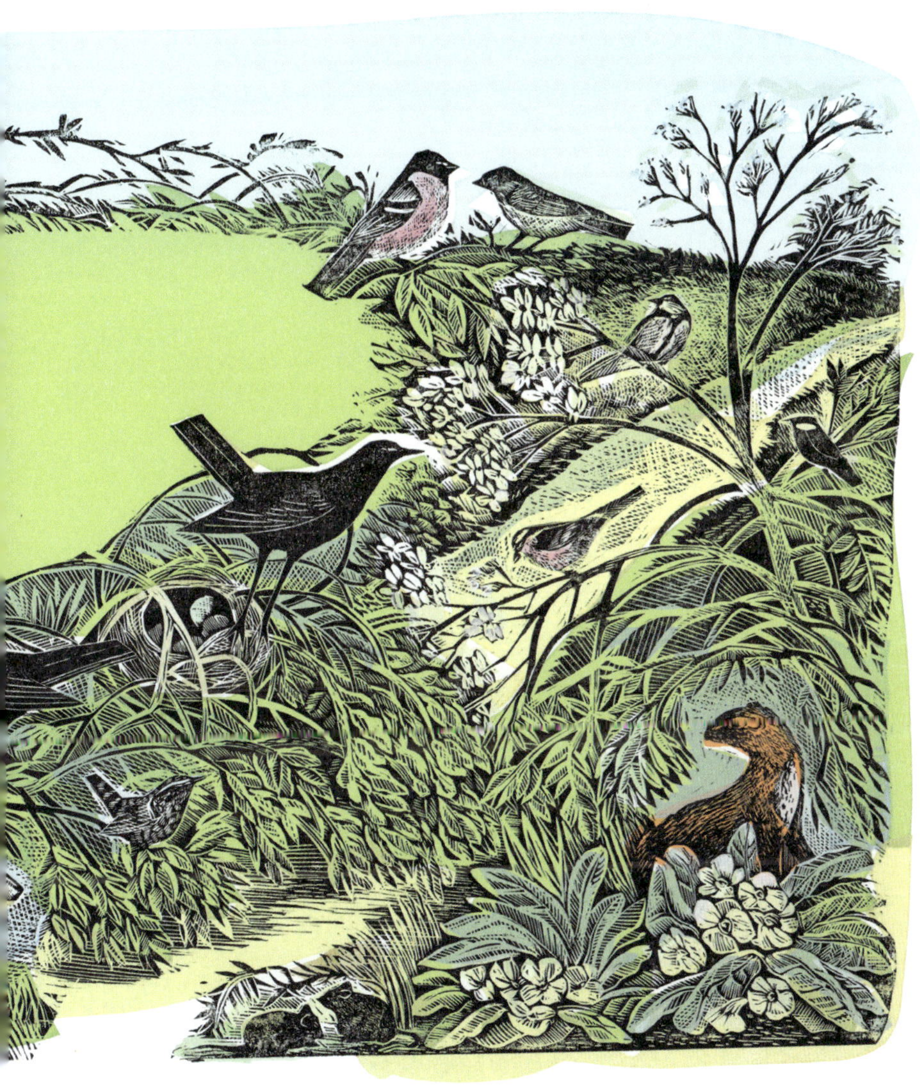

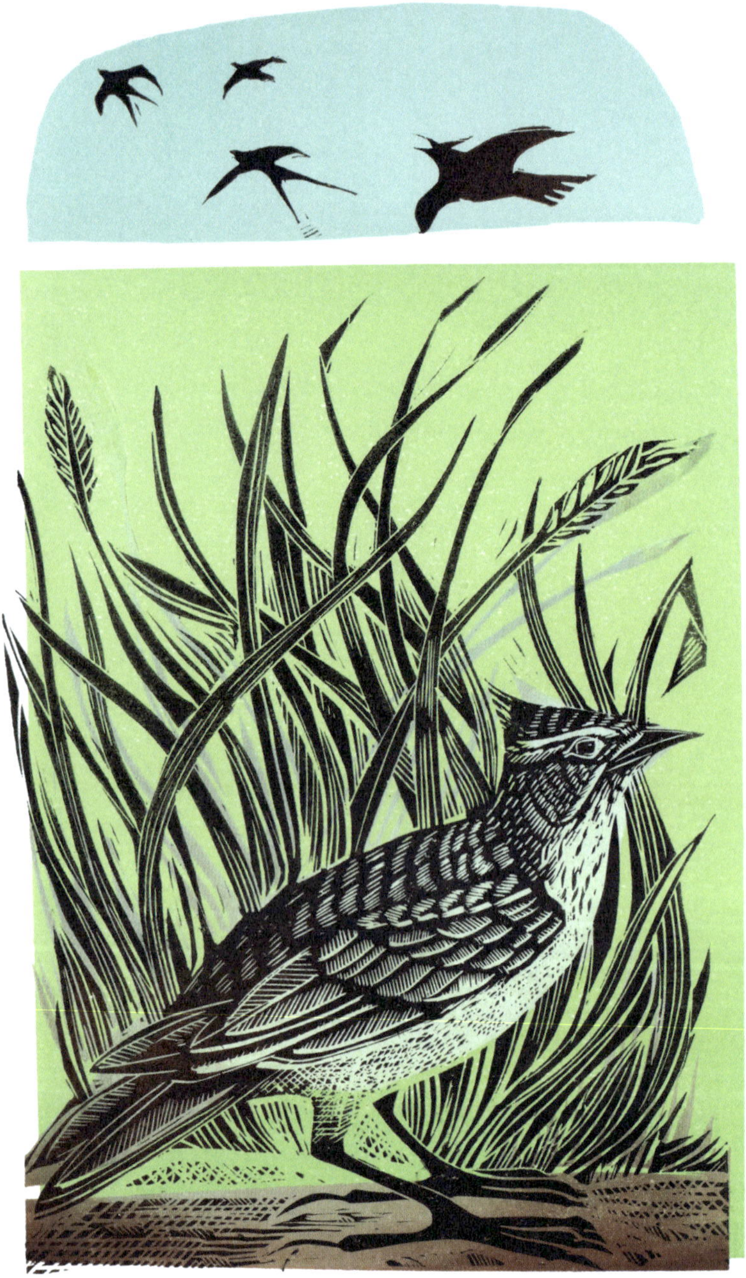

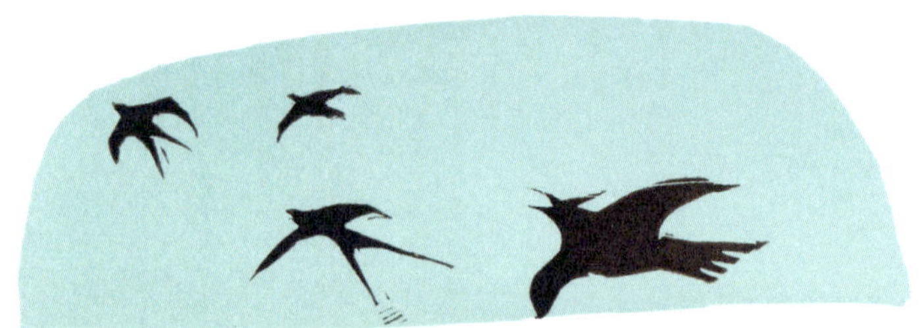

Perhaps the most beautiful song of our local birds is that of the skylark. Growing up in Shropshire on the border of Wales, the sound of the skylarks in the hills was a common one. Skylarks, along with many of our other native birds, have been under threat from modern farming methods, but we still seem to have a good population in Rutland where I now live. It is rather wonderful that on a sunny spring day you can hear the skylark's song from my garden.

Opposite:
Skylark
(Linocut and silkscreen)

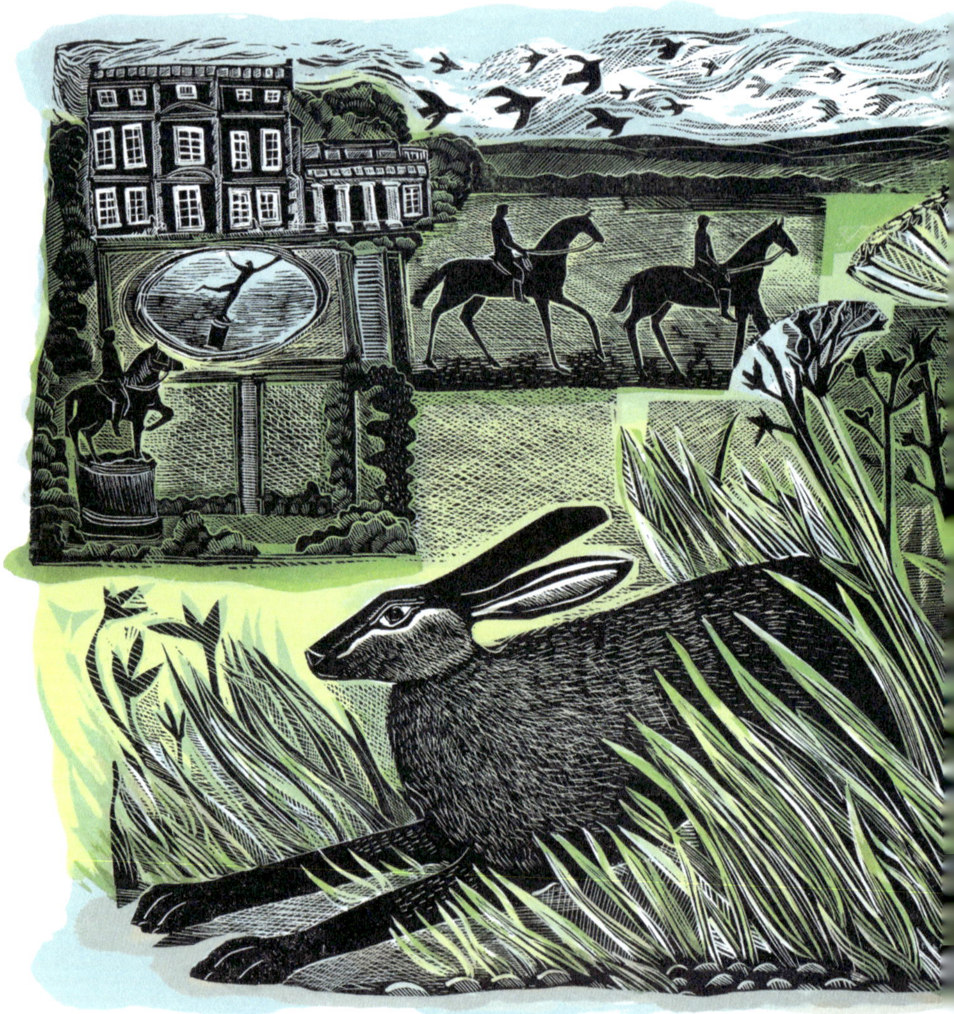

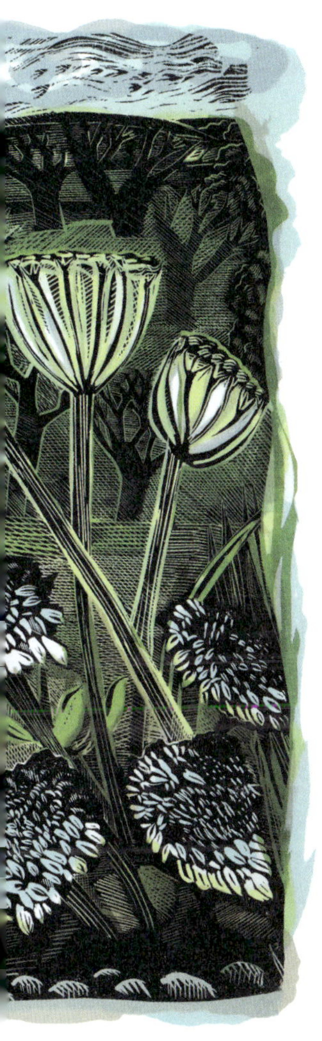

Newby Hall is a place I visited many times as a child with my family. It is always a strange thing to return to these places of childhood as an adult. They are haunted by memories and have a strange feeling as your perspective has changed so much in the intervening years.

Opposite:
Newby Hare
(Linocut and silkscreen)

The 'Shippen Curlew' came from a drawing I did in Shropshire while I was staying with my friends Mary and Hugh Elliot, who run the Twenty Twenty Gallery in Ludlow. As well as exhibiting my work, they have a lovely converted barn that I have stayed in many times. This barn, the Shippen, sits in beautiful Shropshire countryside and I have seen one or two curlews. But it is not like the days when I lived in Shropshire in my youth and there was the constant sound of the curlew's song. It is sad that today the curlews in Shropshire are very much diminished. I see far more of them when I visit the Suffolk coast than I do in Shropshire, but thanks to the charity Curlew Country they are starting slowly to make a comeback.

Opposite:
Shippen Curlew
(Linocut and silkscreen)

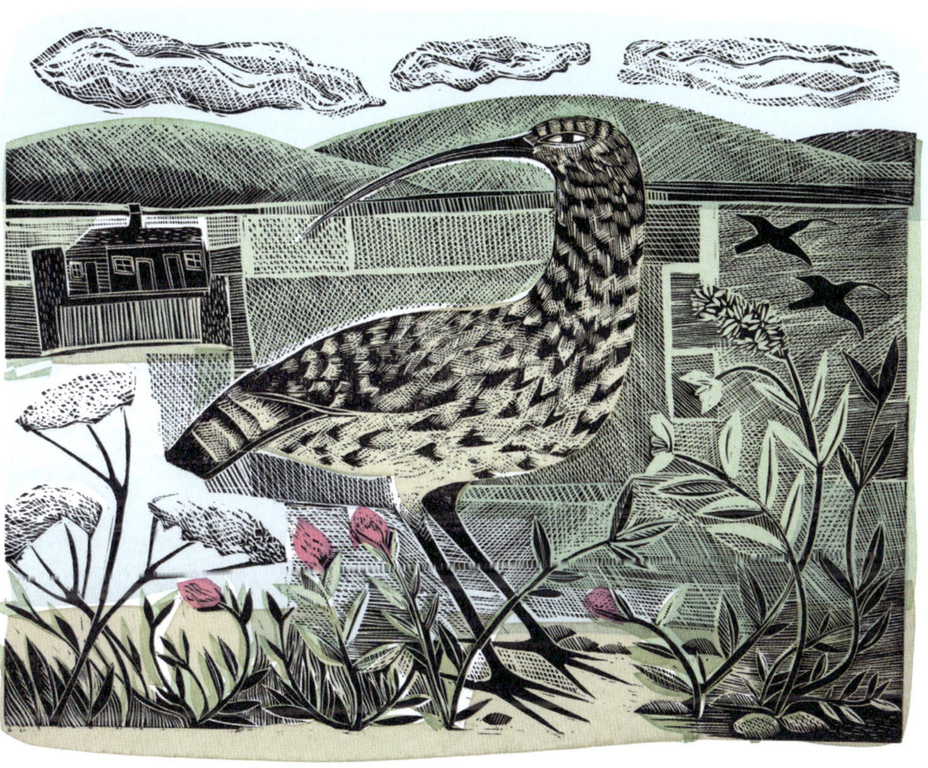

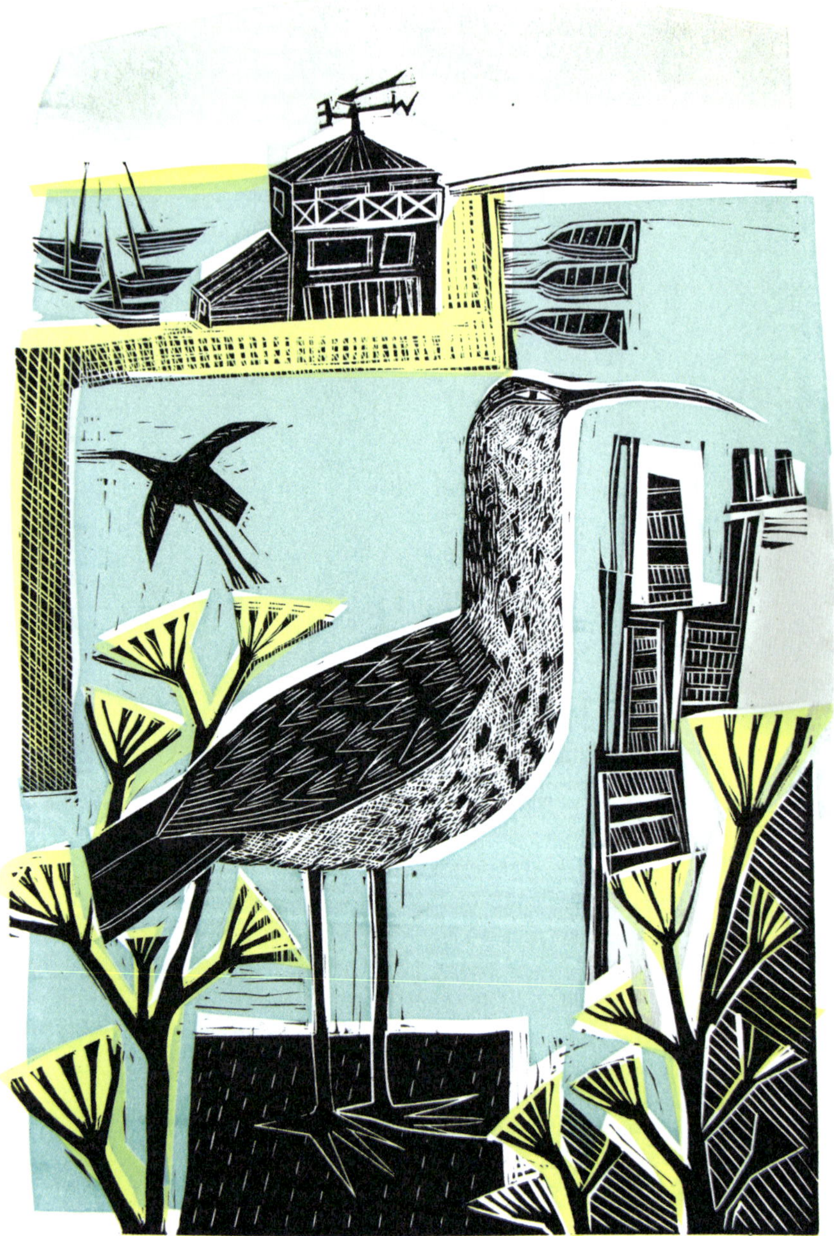

Bent billed, mottled feathers and a song that goes straight to your core: the curlew is a bird that has long fascinated me. In the early 1980s as a student, many of the images I made contained curlews and over the years their presence in my work has not diminished. I find them utterly inspiring. Their song is not a joyous song; it is haunting, melancholic and always moving.

Opposite:
Curlew at Morston
(Linocut and silkscreen)

It is not only their song but their exquisite shape that inspires me.

Opposite:
Two Curlews
(Linocut and silkscreen)

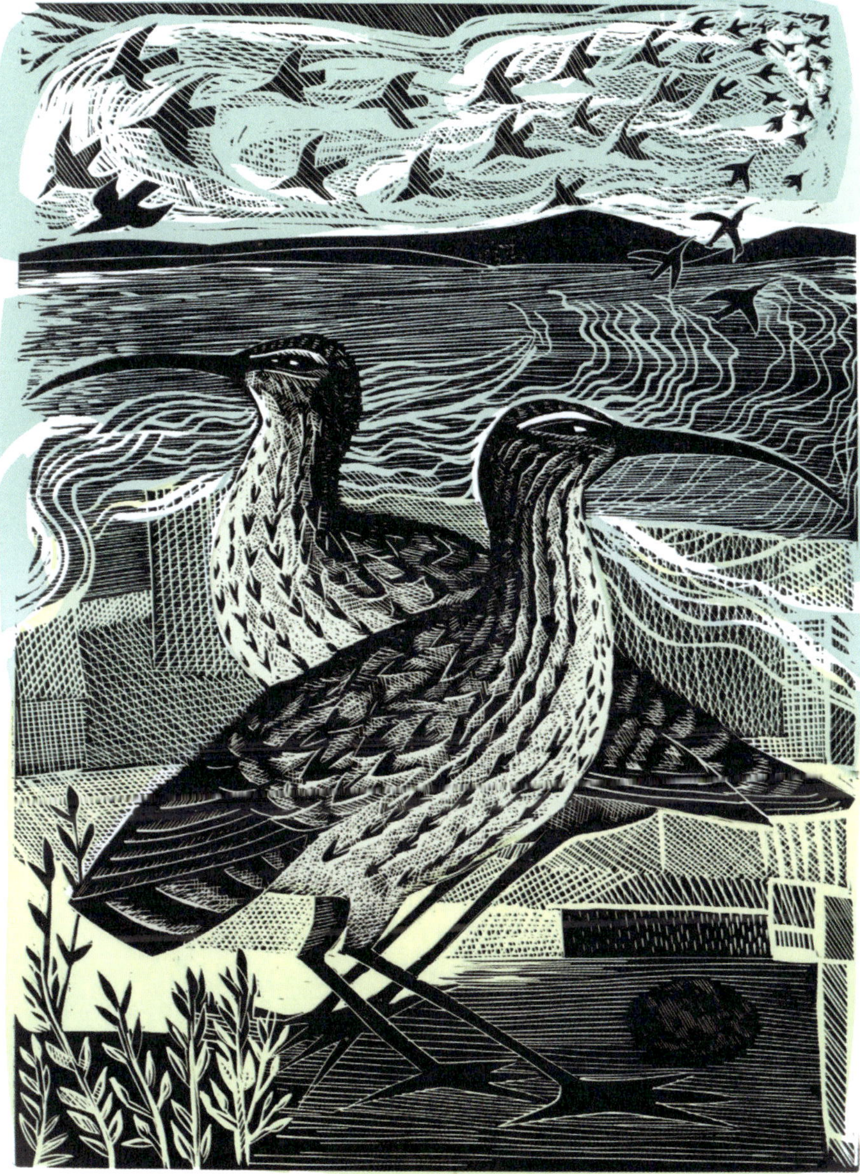

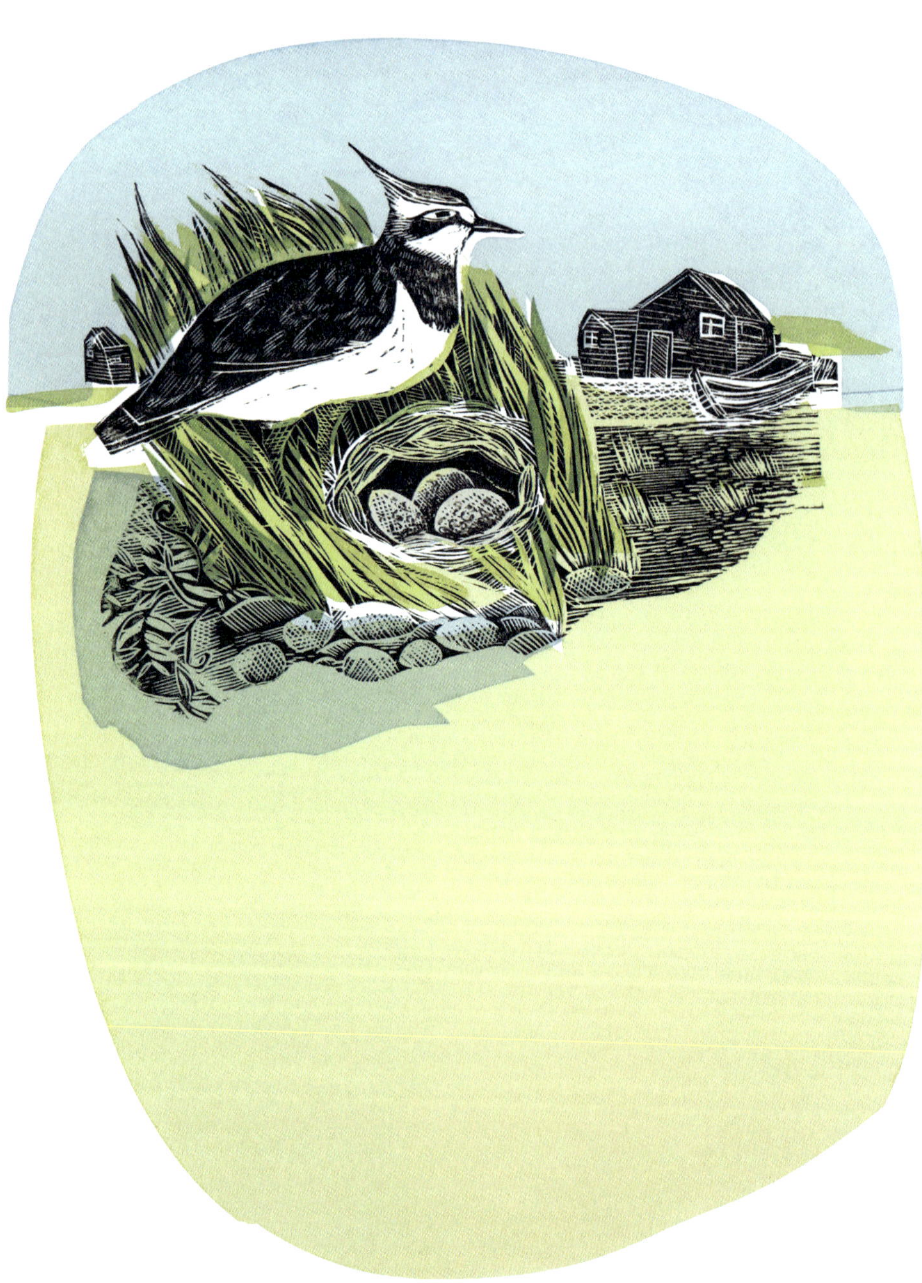

On the sandbank, a large group of lapwings huddle in between sleeping black-headed gulls. The lapwing occasionally fly up with their distinctive call: "pee witt, pee witt!"

Opposite:
Lapwings Nesting
(Linocut and silkscreen)

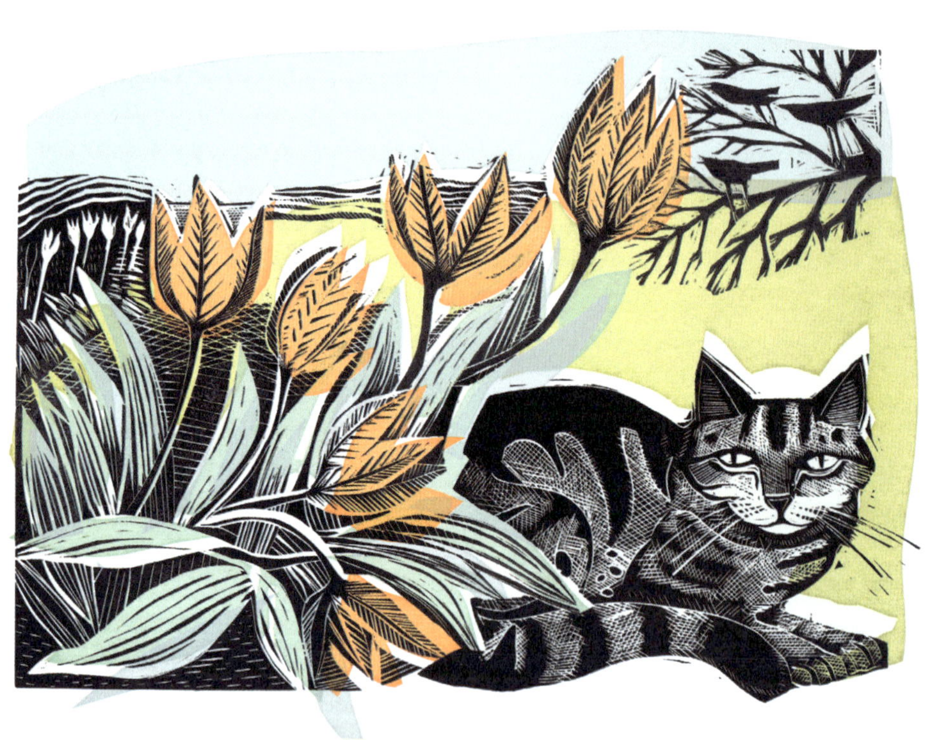

We do not have a cat but there are plenty in our neighbours' houses and they are often to be found hiding in the flower bed on the prowl. This is a worry, but only happens at the front of the house, as, thanks to the whippets, the cats are kept away. Though it doesn't sound like it, I am a cat lover and if it wasn't for the sighthounds and my husband's allergy to their fur, I might have one again. But I am not sure that the comfort of a cat is not outweighed by the death toll to the bird population.

Opposite:
Cat Amongst the Tulips
(Linocut and silkscreen)

*Orford Ness in
Suffolk now has a
thriving population
of barn owls
who often make
their homes in
the abandoned
buildings.*

Opposite:
Barn Owls at Orford
(Linocut and
silkscreen)

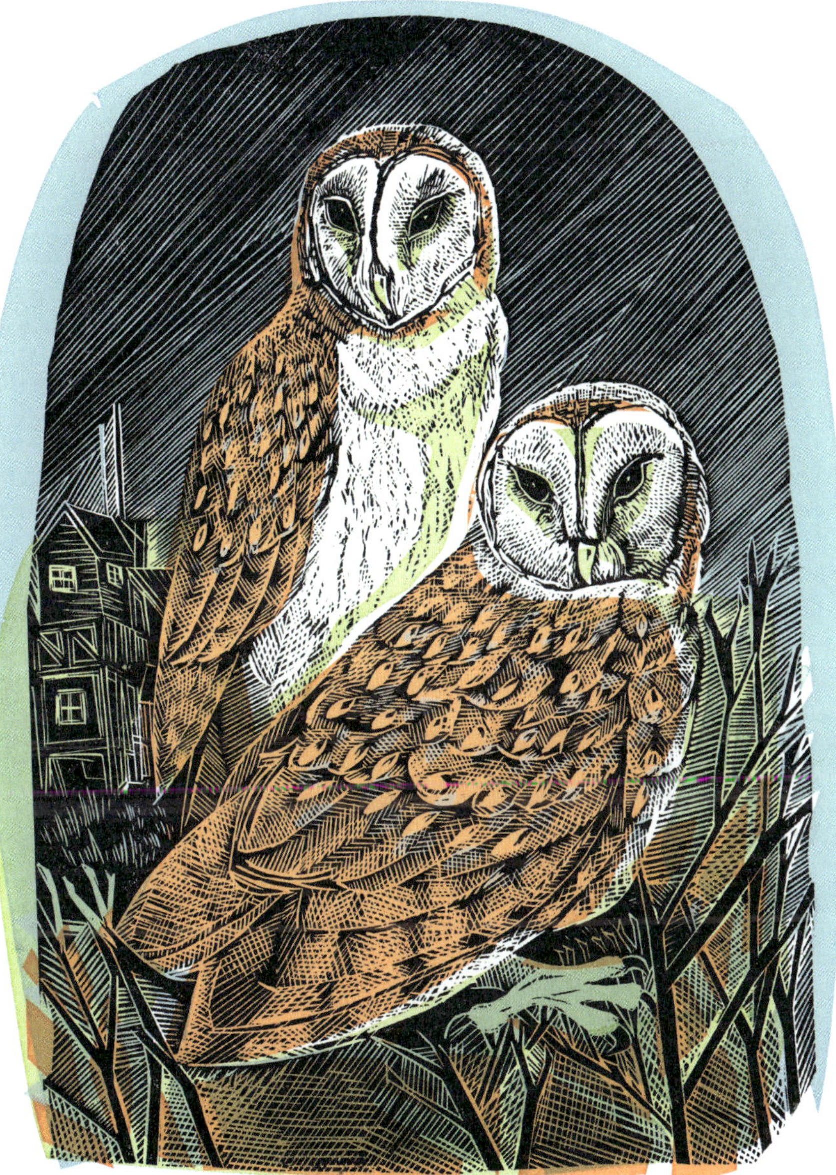

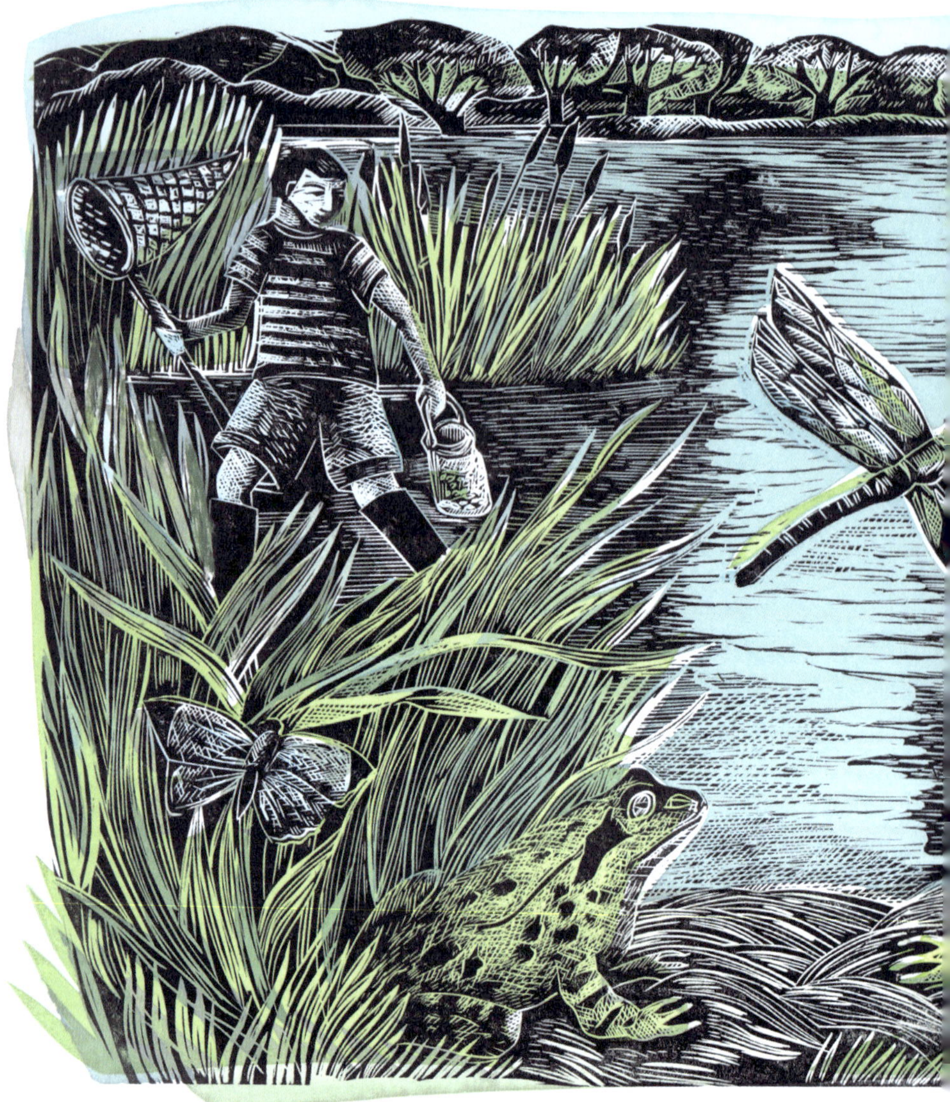

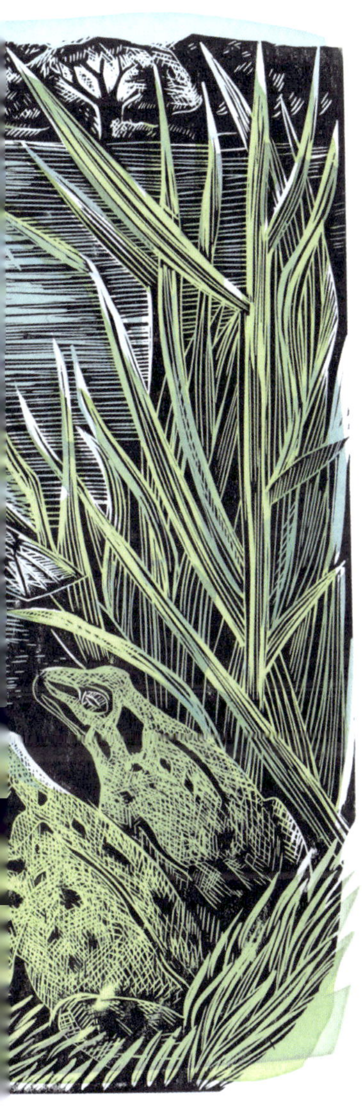

'Death of a Naturalist' is one of Seamus Heaney's most famous poems. There is a rawness to the poem; you can almost smell the still and dank water described. Heaney describes water alive with frogs, in a nature that is so powerful and hypnotic it overwhelms the boy in the poem and changes his perspective of the wildlife around him.

Opposite:
Frog and Flax Dam
(Linocut and silkscreen)

When my husband, Mark, and I are away on our boat Windsong it can't be sunny every day, but I enjoy the spring showers just as much. There is something unbelievably cosy about being told by the weather it is a day to keep still, read a book or do some drawing. The sound of the rain on the boat's roof and the lapping of the waves against its sides is very soothing. Birdwatching in the harbour is also a lovely thing to do; cormorants, herring gulls and swallows are a common sight. One afternoon we saw the less common sight of a cormorant catching an eel. Swallows often sit on the boat lines and you can peer through the portholes and get a close look at them before they launch out once more across the water.

Opposite:
Rainy Days
(Linocut and silkscreen)

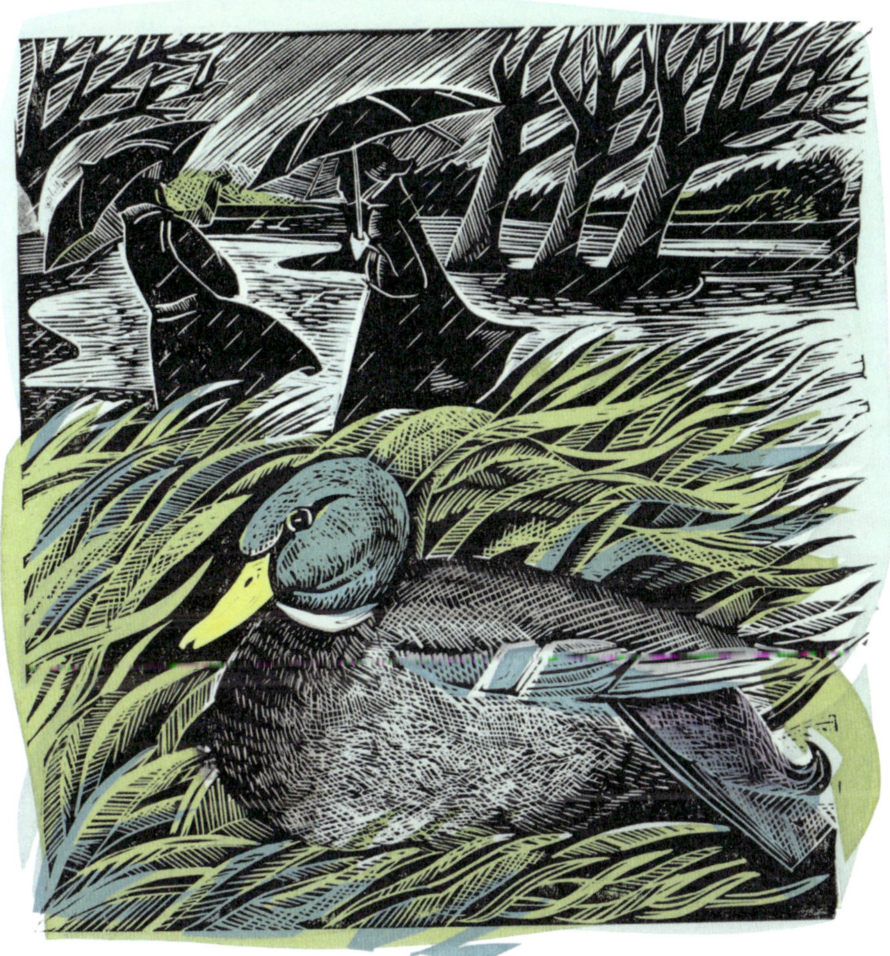

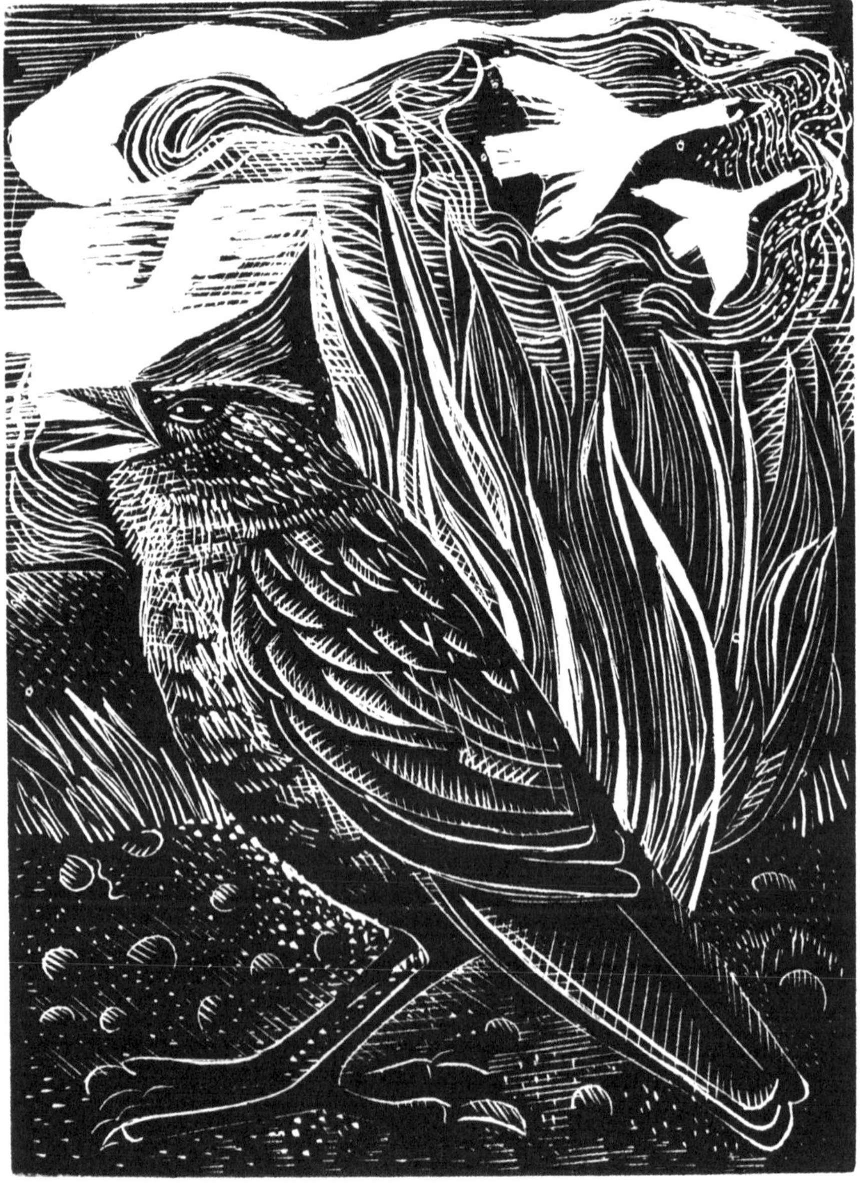

As an art student I was once told a story about how the skylark came to have such a beautiful song. A Russian attendant at Leicester New Walk Museum told me the story and I always think of it when I hear them:

> *God created the earth, and God created Man and that man was Russian. God gave the man all he could want – a family, a horse, a plough and food. One day the Russian said to God, 'I do have all I need to feed my family and work the land, but there is no joy in my world.' So, God bent down and picked up a clod of earth. He then threw the earth into the sky.*
>
> *As the clod rose in the sky it turned into a skylark and began to sing – and created joy. So that is why the skylark sings as it rises higher and higher in the sky and that is why the skylark nests in the soil as it returns to be a clod of earth.*

Opposite:
Skylark
(Wood engraving)

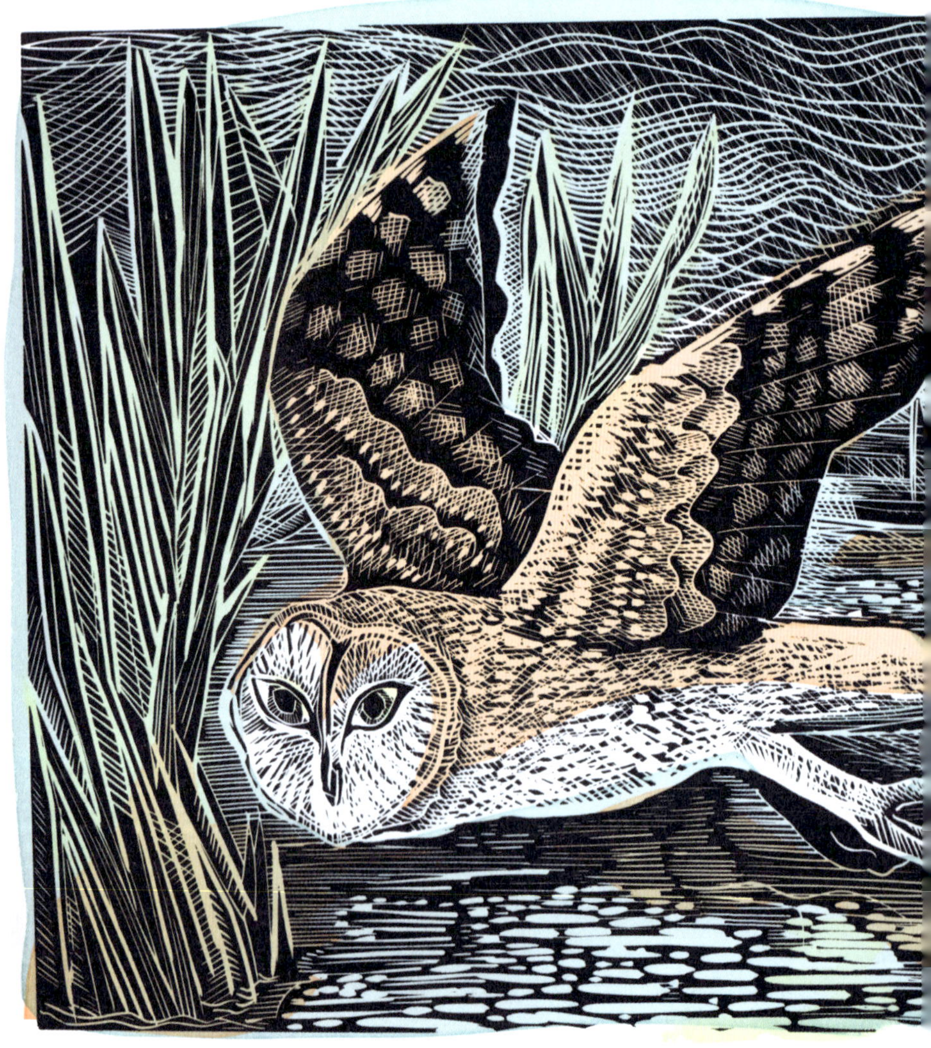

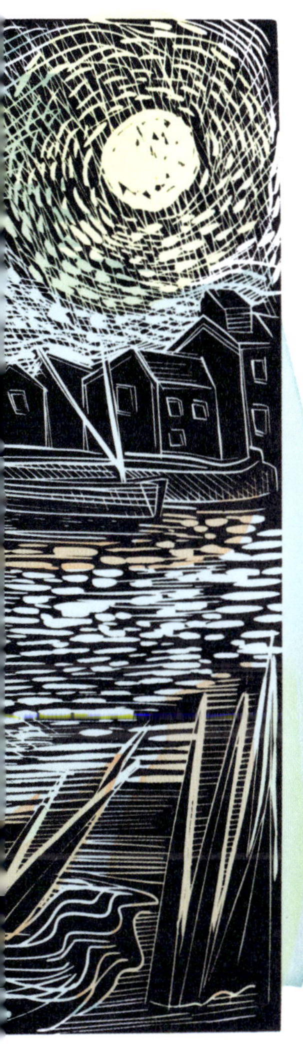

Weaving our way down the river Alde to Snape Maltings in our boat *Windsong* is no easy task. Mark steers, keeping a sharp eye out for the withy sticks that mark the deepest part of the channel. The river changes quickly from a wide stretch of water at Iken to a thin, brown, twisting stream flanked by wide mudbanks. I sit at the back of the boat by the depth gauge, shouting out numbers. These numbers are the amount of water under the keel. When the water depth is less than 4 feet, it gets exciting. But even in *Windsong*, who was built for the Essex rivers, we have to be careful. If we get it wrong, it can mean hours stuck on a mud bank waiting for the tide to turn. But all the tension is well worth it when the sight of the Maltings quayside comes into view. The quay is so beautiful and though the Maltings can be busy, by evening you have the place to yourself. We often spend a few nights there in the springtime. It is the place that inspired my print, 'Marsh Owl'.

Opposite:
Marsh Owl
(Linocut and silkscreen)

Rutland Water is just a short cycle ride from my home, about three miles. The reservoir edge is dotted with bird hides. In the summer of 2016, I did a short residency at the Lyndon side of the nature reserve. This gave me access to watch the ospreys. It was always worth getting there early to enjoy the hides in the quiet, before the crowds of birdwatchers arrive. Like the returning swallows, the returning ospreys mark the end of spring and we are lucky to have them on our doorstep.

Opposite:
Osprey
(Linocut and silkscreen)

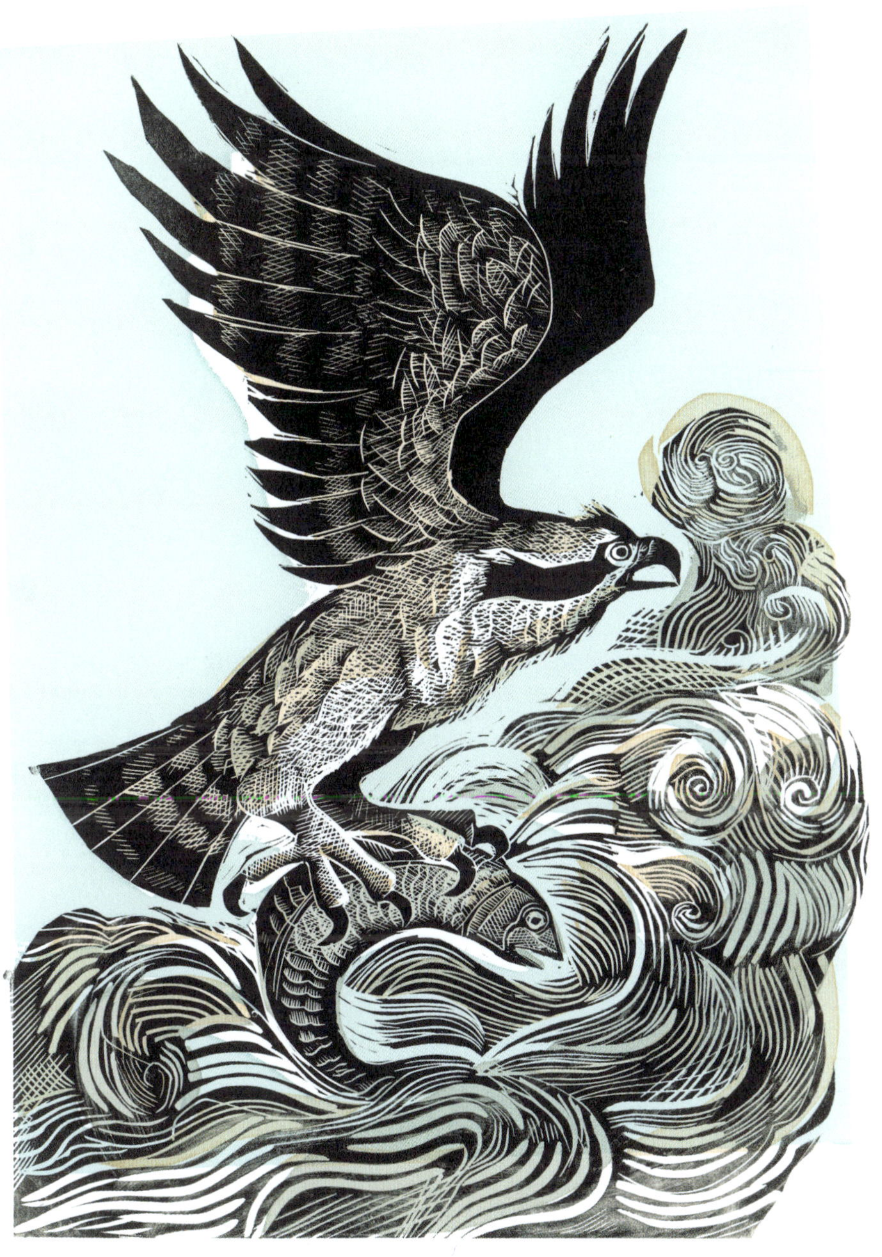

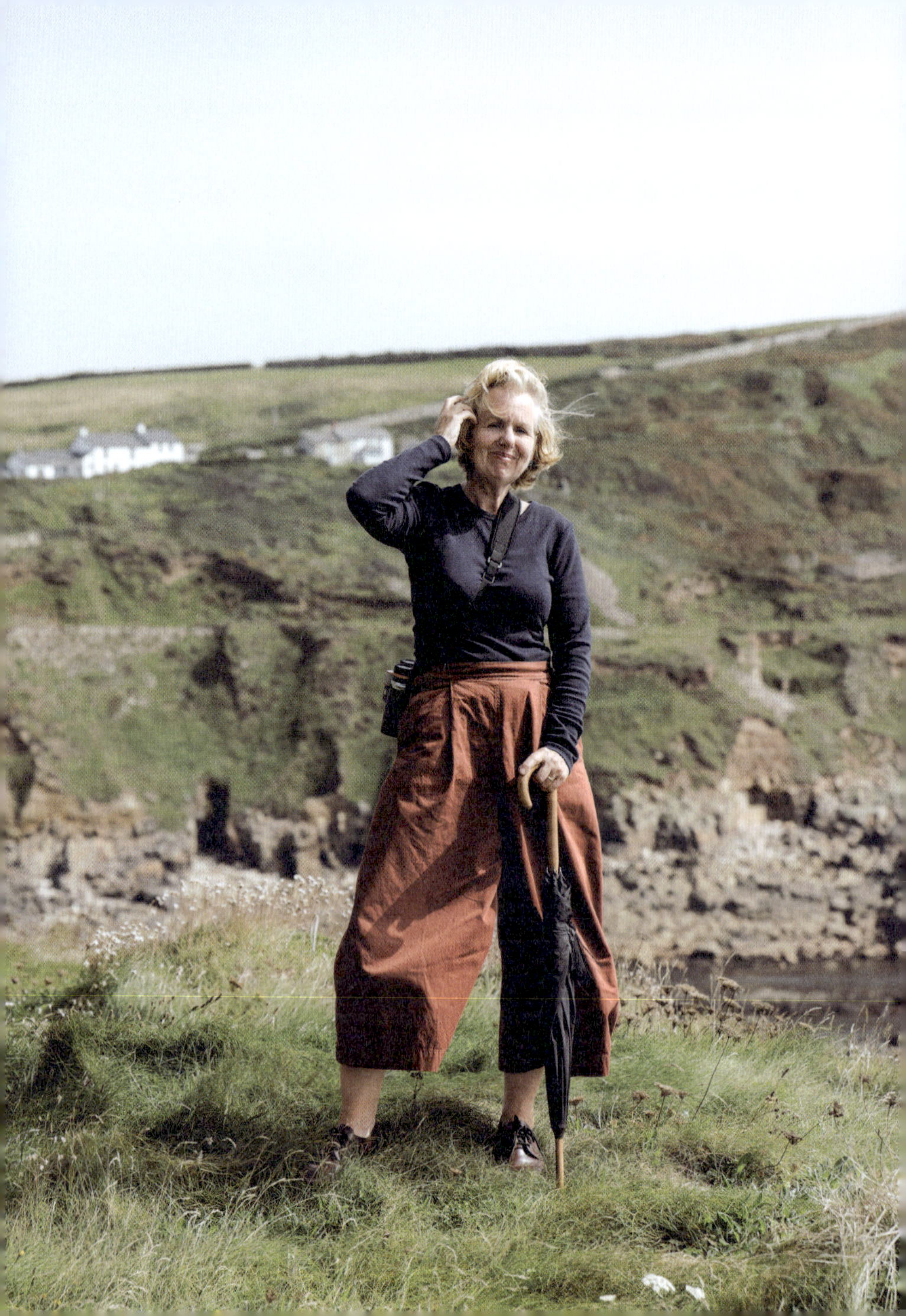

About the Author

ANGELA HARDING lives in the small county of Rutland and works out of the studio at the bottom of her garden in the village of Wing.

Angela has worked on the covers for a number of books including P D James, Ted Hughes, Katya Balen and James Rebanks. Her children's book *RSPB Birds* by Miranda Krestovnikoff was longlisted for the Klaus Flugge prize. Her most recent children's book *Wilding*, by Isabella Tree, was shortlisted for the 2024 Wainwright Prize for Children's Writing on Nature and Conservation. Other recent publications include *Blossomise* by Simon Armitage, a *Sunday Times* bestseller.

Angela has written and illustrated three books published by Little, Brown: *A Year Unfolding*, *Wild Light* and *Still Waters & Wild Waves.*

Angela's unique and distinct style has become instantly recognisable to nature lovers and book lovers alike. Her fans flock to buy her merchandise including calendars, cards, tea towels, tote bags and jigsaws.

She was the 2024 artist for the 'Books Are My Bag' tote bag, celebrating independent bookshops across the UK and Ireland.

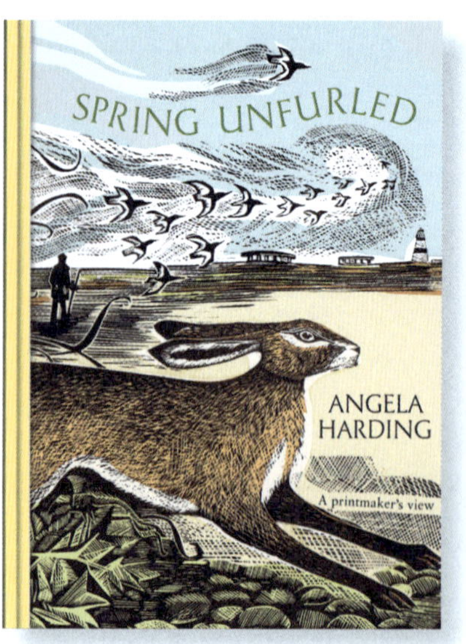

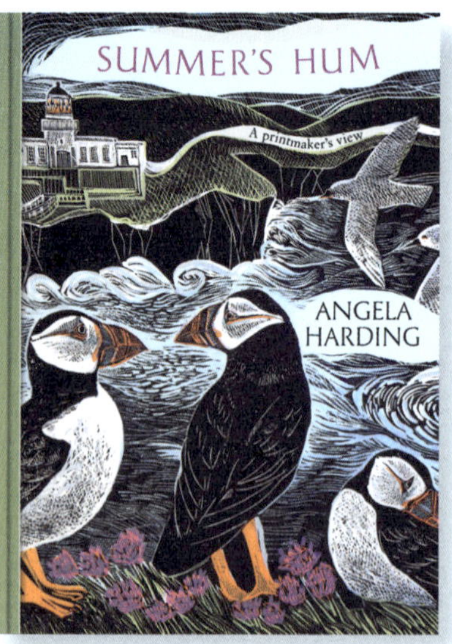

Look out for more books in Angela Harding's Seasonal Quartet series, coming soon

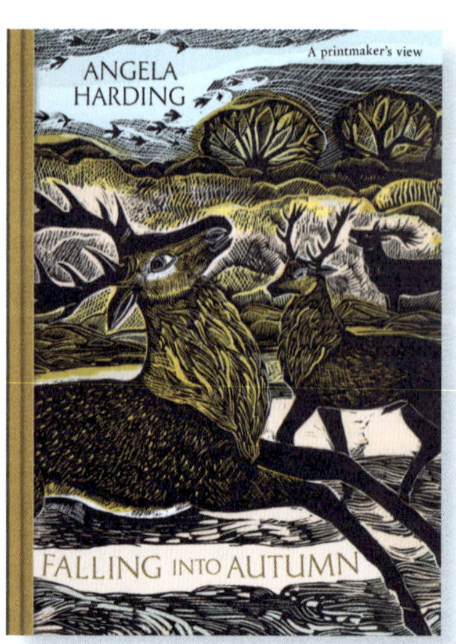

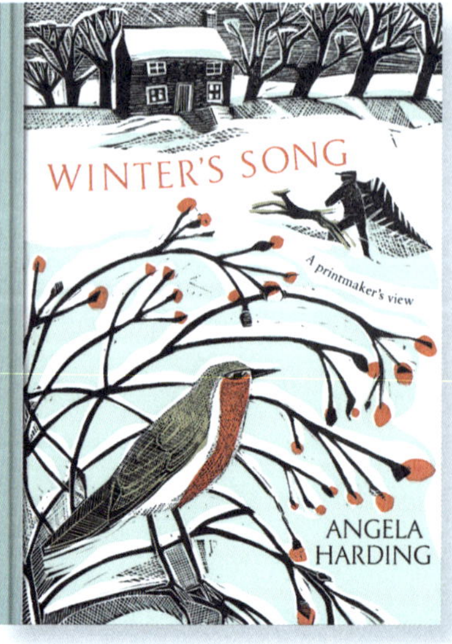

If you enjoyed *Spring Unfurled*, why not explore Angela's other books with Little, Brown

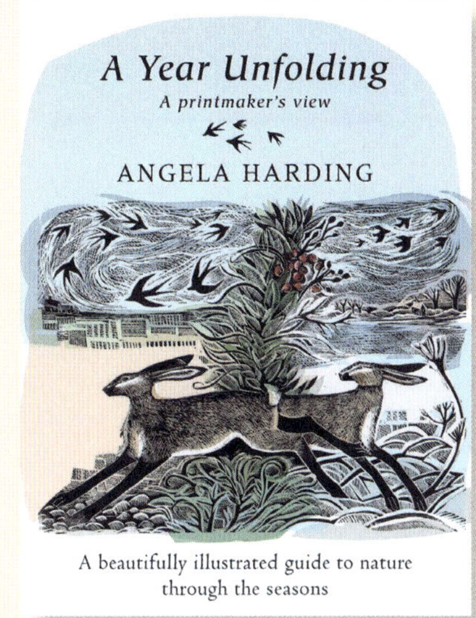

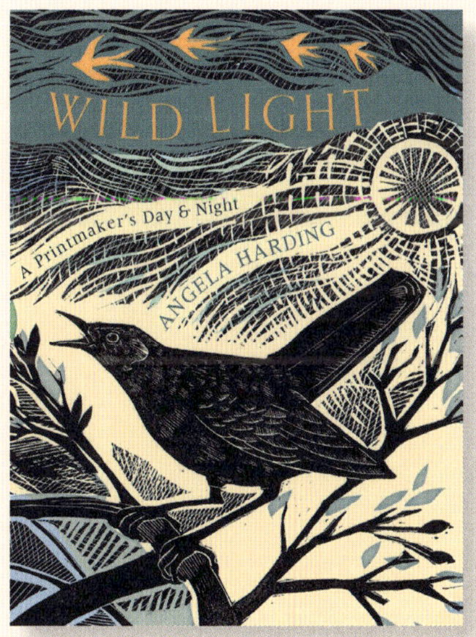

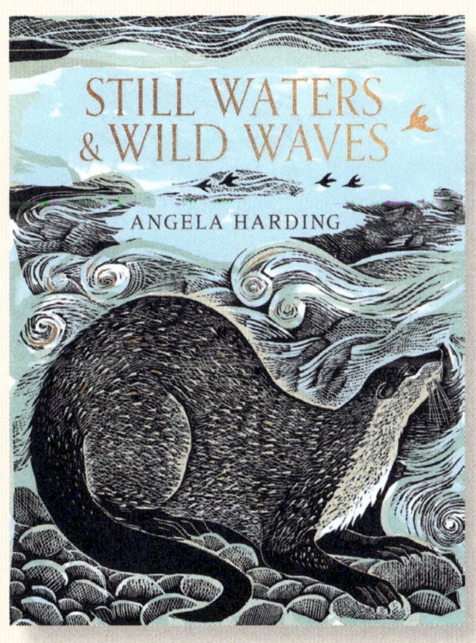

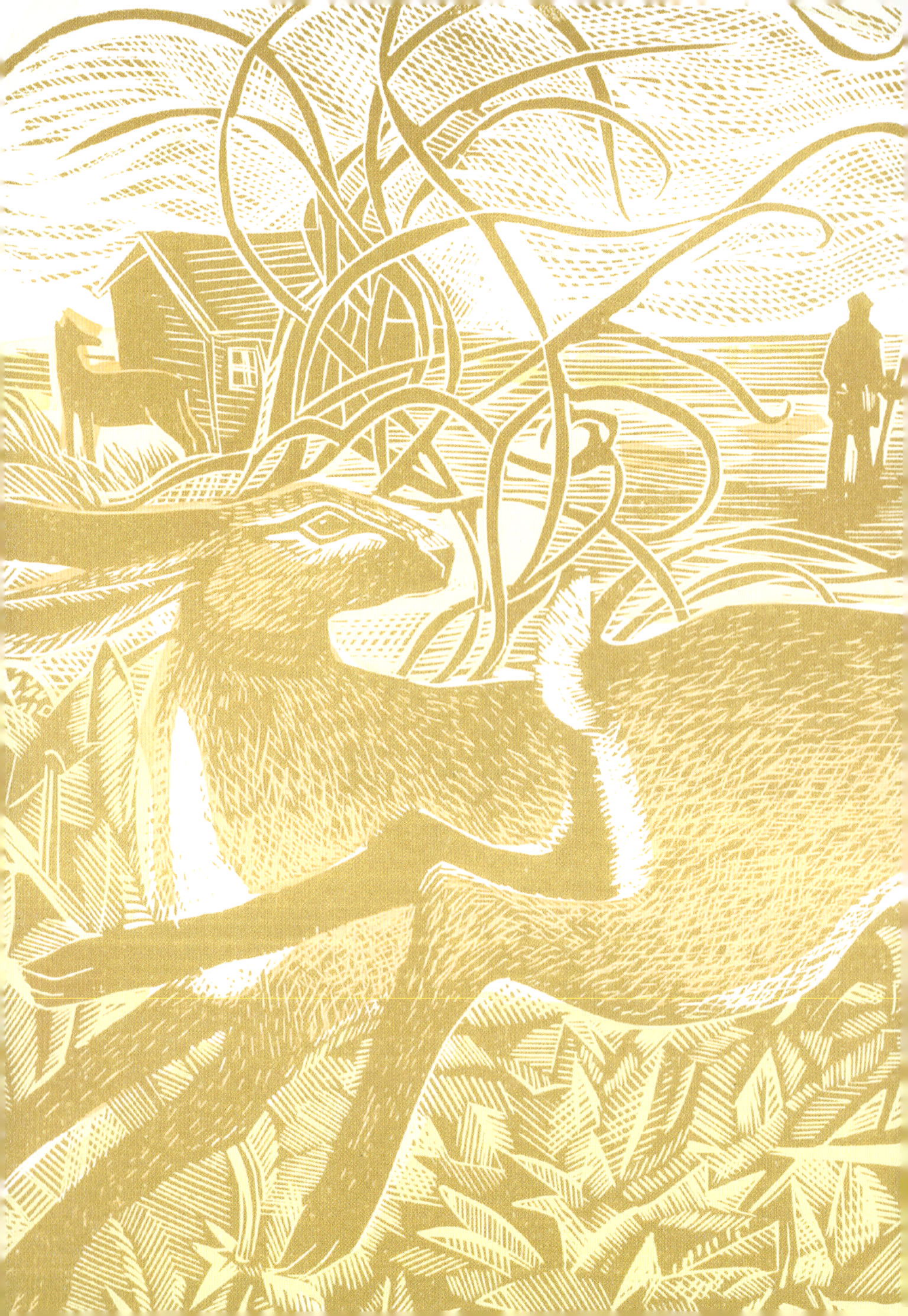